Would You Believe?

Can a Skeptic Find Answers?
An Exploration to Know There is a God, and the
Bible is His Infallible Word.

K. Scott Wells

ISBN: 978-1-7357080-0-3

Acknowledgments

I want to thank my mentors for many years, Dr. Stan Ponz, President of Florida Bible College, and Dr. Wally Morillo, Senior Pastor, Grace Community Church, Pharr, TX, whose support helped make this book possible.

I want to thank Eric Hovind and Creation Today for the education I have received from the study of their material. I also want to thank Ken Ham and Answers in Genesis along with Dr. Henry Morris, the author of the notes and commentary of the "Defender's Study Bible" as well as many other valuable resources. I have obtained much knowledge from their work.

I also want to thank many family and friends for all their contributions and feedback. There are many family members and friends that have contributed in many ways, and I cannot thank them all, but I am very grateful for all my support.

Thanks for purchasing, "Would You Believe?" You may be interested in the workbook designed to help you dive into this information titled, "got faith?"

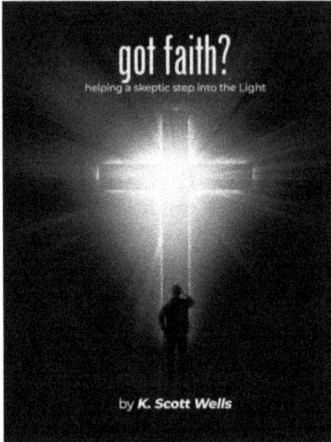

See: https://shop.inspirefaith.net

"got faith?" contains all the same information as "Would You Believe?" but written for the Christan. Plus, it contains a study guide at the end of each chapter and a 90-Day Challenge at the end of the book. This is a great workbook for individuals and small groups.

Table of Contents

Introduction

Are you an atheist? Are you an agnostic? Do you seek the truth? Are you a believer but doubt the veracity of scripture? Are you a Christian who needs your faith strengthened? If you answered "yes" to any of these questions, then this book is for you.

If you are an atheist who has picked up this book, I have two questions for you. The first question is, "Would you admit that you do not have more than 20% of all the knowledge of the universe?"

If you are honest, I would expect you to answer that, of course, you do not possess even 20% of all the knowledge of the universe.

So, my next question is, "Could there be ample evidence to prove there is a god in the 80% of the knowledge you do not possess?" If you are a reasonable person, you would also answer this question in the affirmative. Therefore, you cannot say, "There is no God." You see, to say, "There is no God," you must first have complete knowledge of the universe. If you have a comprehensive understanding of the universe, then you are god. So, either way, the statement is unreasonable.

Perhaps you are simply without knowledge of God, an agnostic. That is fair. Whether you are seeking the truth or trying to strengthen your faith, it is possible the information within this book will help you see evidence for God and perhaps even change the path you are on.

How Did Evolution Know?

Chapter 1

What is evolution? The answer depends on to whom you are talking. An astronomer might speak to you about Cosmic Evolution – the origin of time, space, and matter, for example, the Big Bang. Perhaps he would talk to you about Stellar and Planetary evolution — the origin of stars and planets. Since no one has ever seen a star form, this is all theory. Now, if you talk to a chemist, he may speak with you about Chemical Evolution — the origin of higher elements from hydrogen. However, if you talk with a biologist, this person could talk to you about Organic Evolution — the origin of Life, or perhaps, Macro-Evolution — the changing from one kind of creature into another. Maybe you would talk to someone that would tell you about Micro-Evolution — which is the variations within kinds. This Micro-Evolution (or as I prefer to call it, adaptation) is the only one of these that can be observed.

Let us take a closer look at some of these types of evolution. Stellar evolution is a good place to start. The University of Oregon describes stellar evolution like this:

> Stars form inside relatively dense concentrations of interstellar gas and dust known as molecular clouds. These regions are extremely cold (temperature about 10 to 20K,

just above absolute zero). At these temperatures, gases become molecular meaning that atoms bind together. CO and H2 are the most common molecules in interstellar gas clouds. The deep cold also causes the gas to clump to high

densities. When the density reaches a certain point, stars form.

...the whole process takes about 10 millions years. [1]

We have never seen a star form. Astronomers will say, of course we have never seen a star form. It takes too long. Let's look at some simple math. There are approximately 1,000,000,000,000,000,000,000,000 stars.[2] If the universe is 20,000,000,000 years old, then, that equates to 50,000,000,000,000 new stars a year, or over 95 million new stars every minute. So, to reach the number of stars that exist in the universe, there would need to be 95 million new stars continually forming every minute for over 20 billion years! Yet, we have never seen a star form. Now either the stellar evolution theory is wrong, or the math is wrong. Guess what? The math is not wrong.

Now let us examine Organic Evolution, the origin of life. Organic chemist Alexander Graham Cairns-Smith at the University of Glasgow in Scotland promoted the idea that "mineral crystals in clay could have arranged organic molecules into organized patterns. After a while, organic molecules took over this job and organized themselves."[3] Others have said life started with a lightning strike or volcanic eruption. Livescience.com goes on to say:

"How the primitive Earth cooked up proteins is a chemical mystery. These molecules – vital to biological functions – are made of long strands of hundreds of amino acids, but researchers are unclear how even some of the shortest amino acid chains, called peptides, formed prior to the dawn of living organisms."

Paul Davies, Australian Centre for Astrobiology, Macquarie University, Sydney, admits, "Nobody knows how a mixture of lifeless chemicals spontaneously organized themselves into the first living cell."[4] So, there is not even a functional theory regarding how life got started. The bottom line is, there is no scientific explanation for Organic Evolution.

When most people think of evolution, they think of Macro-Evolution, or as I prefer to reference it, from goo to you by way of the zoo, taken from the book with the same title, "From Goo to You by Way of the Zoo" by Harold Hill. No matter what you call it, evolution is not an entity; it does not know anything; it cannot design; it cannot think; it is not a person or even a being. It is a theory about an unguided process.

Now that we have looked at definitions for evolution, let us look at the definition of science. Webster's Dictionary says science is "Systematized knowledge derived from observation, study, etc." In other words, it is observable and testable.

Is Macro-Evolution either of these? No, it is not. Dr. Mitchell Sogin, an evolutionary microbiologist at the Marine Biological Laboratory in Woods Hole, Massachusetts, believes we evolved from sea sponges. He says, "The sponge is the earliest, most primitive multicelled animal." He also asserts that "Animals and sponges share a common evolutionary history from fungi."[5] Why does Dr. Sogin believe that?

He reasoned that he could examine a limited number of genes that are present in every organism, and by comparing those and counting the differences between them, he could get quantitative measures of the similarities in any two organisms. If the two had

similar gene sequences for a gene that conferred the same trait, he could infer a common ancestry.

So, one could say, "the gene sequences are observable." Yes, that is true, but he uses that data to infer common ancestry. The problem is, similar gene sequences do not prove common ancestry any more than saying these two people have brown hair, so they must have the same parents. Would it not be at least as reasonable to look at the similar gene sequences and conclude they have the same designer?

Is There Time for Evolution?

Time is critical to an atheistic evolutionist. If the world is not billions of years old, evolution does not have time to occur, and the theory loses any notion of being plausible. So, an old Earth is key to evolutionary thinking. Time is the god of atheism.

While there are signs of old age regarding the Earth, what is more important are the limiting factors. I will share three examples of limiting factors regarding the age of the Earth.

The moon is receding from the earth by about 4 cm a year.[6] A receding moon is a huge problem for future humans, but an even bigger one for evolutionists. You see the same math that tells us the moon is getting farther from the earth, and at what rate, can be used to go back in time and tell us how close the moon was to the Earth at a given year.

For example, we can determine how close the moon was to the Earth 4,000 years ago, or (if it existed) 4 billion years ago. Now, evolutionists claim the moon was born about 4.5 billion years ago.[7] However, "If the earth moon system is as old as evolutionists

say, we should have lost our moon long ago."[8] The Inverse Square Law states: The force of attraction between two objects is inversely proportional to the square of the distance between them. So, If the distance is cut by one-third, then the force of attraction between two objects is nine times greater.

As you go back in time, and the moon gets closer and closer to the Earth, the rate at which the moon moves closer to the Earth also increases. Additionally, we must also consider everything the moon affects. The moon controls our tides, affects our wind, the spin of the earth, and even the stability of the earth's rotation on its axis. As the moon gets further away, Earth's rotation slows.

Likewise, if the moon is closer to the Earth, the Earth would spin faster, have stronger winds, and more substantial tidal changes. Life would not be possible on Earth just several hundred million years ago, forget about billions of years ago.

The Inverse Square Law

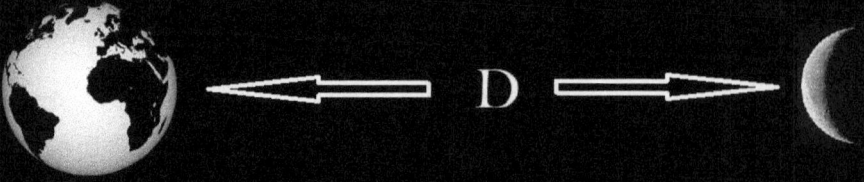

The force of attraction between two objects is inversely proportional to the square of the distance between them.

If the distance is 1/3, the force of attraction between two objects is 9 times greater.
1/3 inverted is 3/1. 3^2 = 9

The next limiting factor is oil pressure. What I am referring to is the underground oil. Remember the BP oil spill in the Gulf? Despite that oil was under tremendous water pressure at a depth of about 5,000 feet, and over 2,000 psi, the oil still came up. It came up because the oil pressure is pressing upwards at almost 10 times that amount, close to 20,000 psi! So, why is this a problem? It is a problem because the rock layers holding down the oil all over the Earth can only hold that kind of pressure for about 10,000 years.[9] Therefore, we know the oil has not been down there for millions of years.

Although there are many others, one more limiting factor for Earth's age is the percentage of salt in the ocean. The oceans are salty and getting saltier due to the water cycle. The water cycle starts with the evaporation of water from the oceans. Clouds form and winds blow them over land. This causes rain to fall on the ground, which washes back into the oceans. This water cycle is not a reversible process, and over time, makes the oceans' salt concentration higher. The problem is that the oceans are only about 3.5% salt.[10] Why is this a problem? Scientists that defend an old age of the earth claim the oceans are about 3.8 billion years old.[11] My point is, if the oceans are billions of years old, they would have a salt content worse than the Dead Sea by now.

You see, just as was the star creation rate illustration, the rate at which the oceans gain salt is simple math. The oceans could go from freshwater to 3.5% salt in less than 5,000 years.[12]

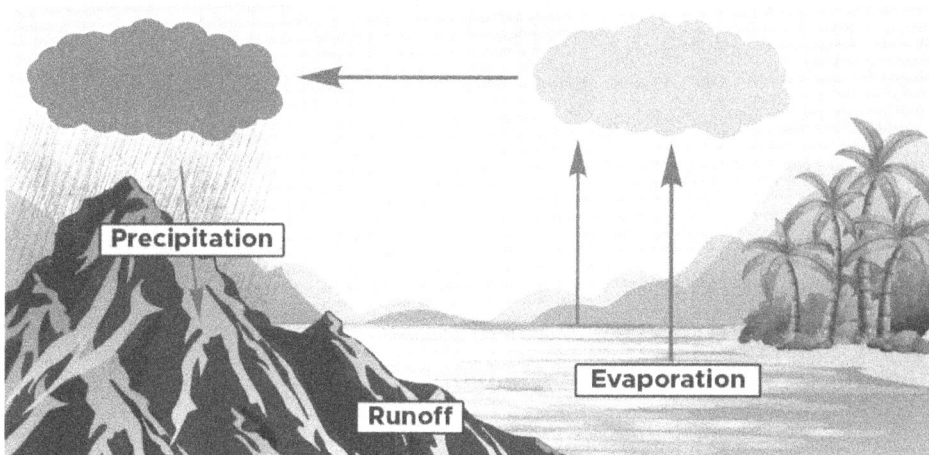

...if the oceans are billions of years old, they would have a salt content worse than the Dead Sea by now.

Looking at just these few scientific facts which limit Earth's age, we can see obvious reasons why the Earth cannot be billions of years old. If the Earth cannot be billions of years old, we cannot have macro-evolution. The theory is impossible.

Genetic Information

However, let us not stop there. Let's look further into macro-evolution to which we will refer to as just "evolution" moving forward. Remember, as I mentioned previously, evolution does not know anything; it is not a designer.

A major problem for evolution is there is no process by which new information is added to the genetic code. Therefore, "survival of the fittest" does not make sense, except within each kind of animal. Let me explain. If there is a herd of animals, and a pack of wolves attacks the herd, they will likely catch the weakest, slowest animal. So, yes, in that example, the fittest survived. However, that is not evolution; no genetic information is added to the gene pool. One could argue that, yes, the animals with the faster longer legs survived, and they will reproduce, and the offspring will also have those traits. Long legs, however, is not indicative of new genetic information being added.

Indeed, information might get lost, but not added. Information on producing offspring with shorter legs would disappear. However, if the herd were deer, they still are deer. Data can only be lost, not gained. This rules out the possibility of evolution.

Some might ask, "What about mutations? Isn't that evolution?" Not if you think evolution makes things better. For every 1,000 mutations, 999 are detrimental or even fatal. Again, we have a math problem. Math is right; evolution does not work.

The Senses

Let us now turn our attention to the human senses, at least four of them.

The Eye

We have two eyeballs to give us depth perception. Our eyes consist of over 200 million working parts.[13] The eye muscles are the most active in the human body. Each eye contains around 107 million light-sensitive cells. The cornea focuses the light. Think of it as a camera lens. The iris of the eye functions like the diaphragm of a camera, controlling the amount of light reaching the back of the eye by automatically adjusting the size of the pupil (aperture). The eye's crystalline lens is located directly behind the pupil and further focuses light. Through a process called accommodation, this lens helps the eye automatically focus on near and approaching objects, like an autofocus camera lens. Light focused by the cornea and crystalline lens (and limited by the iris and pupil) then reaches the retina — the light-sensitive inner lining of the back of the eye. The retina acts like an electronic image sensor of a digital camera, converting optical images into electric signals.

The optic nerve then transmits these signals to the visual cortex — the part of the brain that controls our sense of sight. Six bands of muscles attach to the eyeball to manage the ability of the eye to look up and down and side to side. Three cranial nerves control these muscles. Four of the muscles are controlled by the oculomotor nerve (cranial nerve III), one muscle is controlled by the trochlear nerve (cranial nerve IV), and one muscle is controlled by the abducens nerve (cranial nerve VI.)

All of these parts must work as designed for you to see correctly. Take out one piece, and you cannot see. This complexity raises the question; how could the eye have evolved? However, I have an even deeper one - how did evolution know there was light to see? The problem is, evolution is not an entity. It knows nothing. Some creature cannot decide that light exists and start working on a way to process that light. That is absurd. Evolution is not going to evolve sight because, without a designer, nothing exists to know there is light to be seen. This problem is in addition to the fact that there is still no way for evolution to add genetic information to the genetic code.

The Ear

How about our sense of hearing? How does the ear work? Sound waves cause the eardrum to vibrate. Three bones in the ear (malleus, incus, stapes) pass these vibrations on to the cochlea. The cochlea is a snail-shaped, fluid-filled structure in the inner ear. Inside the cochlea is another structure called the organ of Corti. The basilar membrane of the cochlea contains hair cells. The cilia (the hair) of the hair cells make contact with another membrane called the tectorial membrane. When the hair cells are excited by vibration, the auditory nerve generates a nerve impulse. Then these impulses are sent to the brain. This complexity raises the question; how could the ear have evolved? However, I have an even deeper one — how did evolution know there were sounds to hear?

The Nose

The sense of smell, called olfaction, involves the detection and perception of chemicals floating in the air. Chemical molecules enter the nose and dissolve in mucous within a membrane called the olfactory epithelium. Hair cells are the receptors in the olfactory epithelium that respond to particular chemicals. These cells have small hairs called cilia on one side and an axon on the other side. No one knows what causes olfactory receptors to react; it could be a chemical molecule's shape or size or electrical charge.

The electrical activity produced in these hair cells is transmitted to the olfactory bulb. Then the information is passed on to mitral cells in the olfactory bulb. The olfactory tract sends the signals to the brain to areas such as the olfactory cortex, hippocampus, amygdala, and hypothalamus. This complexity raises the question; how could the nose have evolved? However, I have an even deeper one — how did evolution know there were even scents to be smelled? Only a Designer would know.

> ...that there is still no way for evolution to add genetic information to the genetic code.

The Tongue

You are probably getting my point, but let us take a look at one more. The tongue and the sense of taste. People taste with their taste bud organs. There are approximately 10,000 taste buds in humans. Each taste bud contains 50-150 receptor cells. Receptor cells live for only 1 to 2 weeks and then are replaced by new receptor cells. Each receptor in a taste bud responds best to one of the basic tastes. Two cranial nerves innervate the tongue and are used for taste: the facial nerve (cranial nerve VII) and the glossopharyngeal nerve (cranial nerve IX). The facial nerve innervates the anterior (front) two-thirds of the tongue, and the glossopharyngeal nerve innervates that posterior (back) one-third part of the tongue.

Another cranial nerve (the vagus nerve, X) carries taste information from the back part of the mouth. The cranial nerves carry taste information into the brain to a part of the brainstem called the nucleus of the solitary tract. From the nucleus of the solitary tract, taste information goes to the thalamus and then the cerebral cortex. This complexity raises the question; how could the tongue have evolved? However, I have an even deeper one — how did evolution know there were any flavors to taste?

> **How did evolution know there was light to see, sounds to hear, scents to smell, flavors to taste?**

Science vs Fairytale

You see where there is design and purpose; there is a designer and purpose giver. These things cannot happen by accident. Are you a person of reason, math, science? Great! Use real, observable science, math and logic, to come to the understanding that going from nothing to something, non-life to living, single-cell to human is not science; it is not reality; it is not even possible.

Let's say you have 10 Rubik's Cubes. You scramble them all and place them in a bag. Then you start shaking the bag. What evolutionists believe is like believing the shaking of the cubes will cause them to turn, and eventually, the cubes will all be solved, all at the same time, it just needs enough time.

However, if you think about it, you do realize it will never happen. The only thing that will eventually happen is the cubes will break apart. Then, given enough time, the pieces will ultimately break down and turn to dust. Order will never come from disorder.

If I said, "A frog was kissed and became a prince," then you would rightfully say, "I am speaking about a fairytale." And so it is with evolution. If you exchange the "kiss" with "time," the frog is still not going to become a prince, and you still have a fairytale.

Not only is evolution impossible, but belief in it is harmful. Do you know what motivated Hitler? Hitler believed that the Jews were not fully human, and it would be best to wipe them out. Of course, if you were indoctrinated to believe evolution was true, you could also be manipulated to believe the Jews were pre-human and could, even should, be eliminated.

> However, if you think about it, you do realize it will never happen. The only thing that will eventually happen is the cubes will break apart. Then, given enough time, the pieces will ultimately break down and turn to dust. Order will never come from disorder.

Concentration camps are the fruit of the evolutionary worldview.

Up to this point, we have not looked so much at the evidence for a Creator God, but rather against evolution. However, of course, if there is no evolution, God must exist.

Concentration camps are the fruit of the evolutionary worldview.

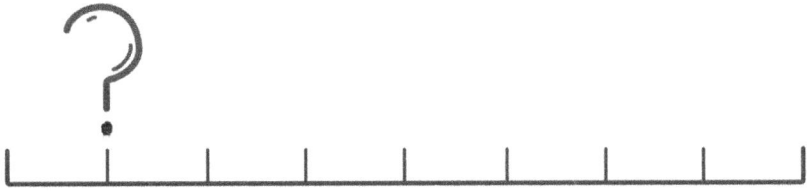

Evidence for God

Chapter 2

Design

Order and design exist in the universe from the cosmic level down to the atomic level. Consider, at the cosmic scale, the relationship of the sun, the moon, and Earth. These three celestial bodies are placed just right for life to occur. If the sun were any closer or any larger, the Earth would be too hot. However, if it was any further away or smaller, then the Earth would be too cold. As mentioned earlier, if the moon were much closer to the Earth or larger, then the Earth would spin too fast, have winds that are too strong, and constant flooding from tides. Conversely, if the moon were too far from the Earth or too small, the Earth would not be stable on its axis, and it would spin too slowly.

Could there be life with a smaller, closer sun, or a moon that is bigger, but farther away? Yes, but notice that the moon is 400 times smaller than the sun, but also 400 times closer, resulting in a moon and sun that appear the same size. The moon is able to block the sun perfectly in an eclipse. That does not impact life or death, but here is my point. God did not just set up the size and position of the sun, moon, and Earth in any random configuration that could sustain life, but in a manner that reveals Him and His creation. Since the moon can give us a perfect eclipse of the sun, we are able to learn about the sun and understand its makeup much better than we could if solar eclipses never occurred. So, God did not setup the solar system in just anyway that would allow for life, but in a way that would also allow for us to learn about His creation.

What about systems within the Earth? Earth has oxygen, carbon dioxide, plants, and animals. The plants take in carbon dioxide and produce oxygen. At the same time, the animals take in oxygen and produce carbon dioxide.

Plants and animals must exist, wholly functional, and at the same time, or we do not have life.

Let us turn our focus to the microscopic. Frank Sherwin, M.A., stated the following:

> For the cell to remain alive, there must also be a constant exchange of materials from the outside of the cell to the inside, and vice versa. For example, among many other ions, potassium is critical for cellular function and homeostasis. A precisely shaped and charged potassium gate found in the cell membrane is known to have a latch that rotates much like an iris! It also has switches and pulleys. Working in exquisite harmony, the four principal parts of the gate—collectively called the Kir channel—are designed to selectively allow millions of potassium ions per second to pass through the gate while keeping out legions of pesky gatecrashers (other ions).[14]

Take a moment to appreciate the complexity of this. When Darwin wrote his book, "On the Origin of Species by Means of Natural

Selection, or the Preservation of Favoured Races in the Struggle for Life," (By the way, I am willing to bet most of my readers have never seen the full title of this book. It is not usually written in full because then people would recognize the racism that is intertwined with evolutionary thinking.) he assumed that as things got smaller, they also became simpler. An understanding of the intricacies of DNA and cellular function was still more than a century away from discovery. Darwin had the excuse of ignorance. We do not.

Anthropic Principle

The word "anthropic" is used to relate to human beings or their existence. The Anthropic Principle is the principle that the universe appears to be fine-tuned for human existence. The idea is that the universal constants in the universe (such as the universal gravitational constant, strong/weak nuclear force, speed of light, electromagnetic force, photon mass, etc.) seem to be "finely-tuned" to allow for our existence.[15]

The Kalam Cosmological Argument says, "Everything that begins to exist has a cause. The universe began to exist. Therefore, the universe must have a cause." God is the first cause, the only thing eternal.

Laws of Logic and Nature

There are laws of logic such as, "You cannot have "A" and not have "A" at the same time in the same relationship." That is something referred to as the law of noncontradiction. We also have laws of nature, such as $E = mc^2$. Not only do these laws of logic and nature exist, but they are simple to understand, to study, describe mathematically. How do these simple laws of logic and nature exist if there is no lawgiver? God not only created these laws, but he did so in such a way that we can easily discover and understand them. Order and laws exist in the universe because there is an order and lawgiver.

While one can examine the realms of logic and science, and find God, perhaps the best evidence for God, is in the domain of human experience. God changes lives every day and interacts with people regularly, not just in the Scriptures. I can give you one such example from my own life.

Life Experiences

When I was living in Tucson, I experienced God in a situation that will likely never occur again in my life. Looking back, I can see that He set up all the right circumstances, so things could "fall into place." My wife, Maria, is a nurse and often worked on the weekends. At the time, we just had two children. They had stayed overnight with their grandparents on Saturday night. Alone Sunday morning, I had overslept a little and was running late for church.

On my way, I stopped for a red light. A man walked on the crosswalk in front of me, came over to my window and asked me for a ride. Up until this point in my life, I had never picked up a hitchhiker, but I had an overwhelming thought to tell him, yes, and I did. I am sure that if someone had been with me, I would have said no. He asked me if I could take him to an intersection just a few miles down the road and the direction I was heading. I agreed to take him.

He saw the way I was dressed and asked me if I was going to church. I told him I was. He wanted to know where that was, and I mentioned that it was towards the center of town. It was a few miles further than where he stated he wished to go. He said that it was closer to where he wanted to be and asked if I would then take him that far. I asked him where he needed to get to, and he said, "Grant and Alvernon."

Now, to go from where we started to Grant and Alvernon is several miles into the middle of Tucson. He mentioned he was trying to get a Bible class there but was fine with me just taking him part of the way. He then proceeded to tell me how he messed his life up with drugs, and because of the drug abuse, he was recently thrown out of his house. He was trying to straighten his life out and, at that time, was going to a Bible study group for help and support.

We arrived at my church, and I invited him to join me. He did not want to do that. He really wanted to get to his Bible study group. If I let him go, he would need to start hitchhiking again, and Jesus said if someone asks for you to walk with him one mile, then walk with him two. That is a paraphrase of Matthew 5:41. So, I took him the rest of the way.

When we got there, we were pretty early for his class. He started hitchhiking early, not knowing how long it would take. I asked him if we could pray. He said we could. I just wanted to know a little more information before we prayed, so I asked him if he knew what it meant to be a Christian. He said he knew Christ but had fallen away. We started to pray, and when I finished praying for him, he was in tears. He asked me how I knew what to say and what he needed. I told him it was not me praying, but the Holy Spirit praying through me.

I was blown away as he then explained how right-on the prayer was. He shared details of his life that I prayed about, but that he had not previously shared. When he finished sharing, he saw some other people from his class pull up and said he would be fine now and thanked me for my time and the prayer and went to his class.

By then, I missed my church service, but that experience far exceeded the experience of a typical Sunday morning service. I was able to use the wisdom that could have only come from God to bless someone that I will likely never see again. Plus, I was blessed. I listened to God, and my obedience to Him caused me to receive a blessing in a way I will never forget. That experience is not one that anyone can dispute. It is my experience, and I do not need to *believe* God is real, I *know* He is real.

> ...when I finished praying for him, he was in tears. He asked me how I knew what to say and what he needed. I told him it was not me praying, but the Holy Spirit praying through me.

That experience is my experience, but there are countless other experiences by numerous other people, that point to God. Talk to other Christians, read their stories in books, magazines and on the internet. The Holy Spirit is actively at work among His people.

God's Origin

Some may ask, "Where did God come from?" However, God did not come from anywhere. As I mentioned above, God is the first cause. God has no beginning or end. He is the Alpha and the Omega (beginning and the end). He is outside of time/space/matter. He created time/space/matter. As Einstein proved, these three things are inseparable and must be created together. If you had matter but no space, where would you put it? If you had matter and space but no time, when would you put it? In the very first verse of the Bible, we see this happened all at once. "In the beginning" (the creation of time), "God created the heavens" (space) "and the earth" (matter).

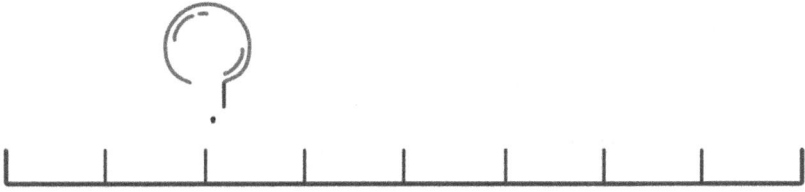

The Bible's Authenticity

Chapter 3

Now that I have brought up the Bible, let us take a closer look at what the Bible is. First of all, what does the word "Bible" mean? The word is a Greek derivative from "biblion," which means scroll, or little book. Biblion is derived from biblios, and this is the inner bark of the papyrus plant, a kind of reed grown in warm climates like Egypt, and from which the ancient people made writing material. It can refer to any book or scroll made from this bark. Later, the word was used to describe any book regardless of the material. The term, biblios, is the first word in the Greek New Testament (Matthew 1:1).

Jerome, (27 March 347 – 30 September 420), a theologian and historian, called the Bible, "the Divine Library" around 400 AD. From 400 AD to the 13th Century, the Greeks and others began to call it "The Books above all other books." Then it was singularized to "The Book" of books. Today we have the Anglicized Greek word, the Bible.

What Is It?

The Bible is, "...the collection of books of the Old and New Testament Scriptures recognized by and used in Christian churches."[16]

It is "...the embodiment of divine revelation, and that the records which contain that revelation are genuine, credible, canonical, and supernaturally inspired."[17]

"It is here asserted that the BIBLE claims for itself that on the original parchments every sentence, word, line, mark, point, pen-stroke, jot or tittle was placed there in complete agreement with the divine purpose and will. Thus, the omnipotent and omniscient God caused the message to be formed as the precise reproduction of His Word. The original text was not only divine as to its origin but was infinitely perfect as to its form. It is both necessary and reasonable that God's Book — the Book which He is the author, and which brings revelation and discipline of heaven down to earth — shall, in its original form, be inerrant in all its parts. It is called the Sacred Scriptures by way of eminence" (John 7:42; 5:39; 2 Timothy 3:15).[18]

I like to identify the BIBLE as being for us:

God's Basic Instructions Before Leaving Earth!

The following list provides us with a few major characteristics of the special, unique book we call the Bible.

• The Bible is represented as one book.

• Inside, there are 66 books recorded by many human writers; or another way to view it is as 66 chapters recorded in one book, inspired by one God.

• The book conveys one central theme — Redemption.

• In Genesis 1:1, God divinely gave us an important doctrine of Christianity, the Trinity. It is often missed when reading our English Bible. In the English language, singular means one, and plural means two or more. However, in the Hebrew language, singular means one, dual means two, and plural means three or more. The word "God (Elohim)" is the plural form meaning three or more. "In the beginning God (we — three or more) created the heavens and the earth."[19]

• In Genesis 2:4, the English Bible has the word LORD which signifies the personal name of God is the one translated. This personal name, Jehovah, means "God who saves."

• In Revelation 22:13 cf. 16-17,21, we read that Jesus Christ offers redemption to any who will receive it by faith alone in Christ.

• The unity found in the Bible was recorded over a span of approximately 1500 years (1450 BC to 100 AD).

• In 2 Timothy 3:16; 2 Peter 1:21; 2 Samuel 23:1,2; Acts 1:16; 28:25 we read the book has one author — the Holy Spirit.

• And the miraculously unified book had approximately thirty-five human writers.

The Scribes

The previous pages provide a basic definition and description of the Bible. One of the most common misconceptions regarding the Bible is that it came to be after a long game of "Telephone." Perhaps you are not familiar with this game. In "Telephone," you sit in a circle, one person writes some phrase or description down on a piece of paper, then whispers what they wrote down to the first person. That person whispers it to the next person and so on. By the time you get to the last person, the last person states what they heard, and it never matches what the first person wrote down.

So, how do we know what we have today is what God originally intended? Well, the following describes the process the ancient scribes used to copy the Word of God. What you are about to realize is they were exceedingly meticulous in their job. Here are some of the rules they followed:

• The scroll must be the skin of a clean animal.

• Each skin must contain a specified number of columns, equal throughout the entire book.

• The length of each column must extend no less than forty-eight lines and no more than sixty lines.

• The column breadth must consist of precisely thirty letters.

• The space of a thread must appear between every consonant.

• The width of nine consonants must be inserted between each section.

• A space of three lines had to appear between each book.

• The fifth book of Moses (Deuteronomy) had to conclude exactly with a full line.

• Nothing – not even the shortest word – could be copied from memory, it had to be copied letter by letter.

• The scribe must count the number times each letter of the alphabet occurred in each book and compare it to the original.

• If it was determined that a manuscript contained even one mistake, it was discarded.[20]

There is no modern profession that compares to the meticulous nature as that of the ancient scribe. In fact, when the Dead Sea Scrolls were discovered in 1946, we were able to see that the manuscripts we have today to translate into modern languages match exactly the manuscripts of a 1,000 years earlier. [20]

Dr. F. F. Bruce, Rylands Professor of Biblical Criticism and Exegesis at the University of Manchester, is one of the world's foremost authorities on the New Testament. In his book, *The Books and the Parchments*, he writes: "There is no body of ancient literature in the world which enjoys such a wealth of good textual attestation as the New Testament."[21]

Dr. Bruce states that the Septuagint (the Greek translation of the Hebrew Old Testament written about 200 BC) helps to establish the reliability of the Old Testament's transmission through 1,300 years when compared with the Masoretic Text (916 AD) we have today.

There are thousands of existing manuscript copies of both the Old and New Testaments and there is an amazing agreement. There are many more manuscript copies of the Bible than existing manuscripts of ancient secular writers such as Homer and Josephus. This fact additionally validates authenticity and accuracy. We can confidently proclaim that what we have today is what God originally intended.

The Truth

How do we know the Bible is the truth? It is one thing to say that what was originally written down is what we have today. However, it is an entirely different matter to say that what was originally written down was the truth. Consider the following points.

Eyewitness Accounts

The writers of the New Testament wrote as eyewitnesses or recorded eyewitness accounts. Furthermore, the events recorded were presented in front of hostile witnesses as found for example in Acts 2:22-24.

"Men of Israel, listen to these words: Jesus the Nazarene, a man attested to you by God with miracles and wonders and signs which God performed through Him in your midst, just as you yourselves know— 23 this *Man*, delivered over by the predetermined plan and foreknowledge of God, you nailed to a cross by the hands of godless men and put *Him* to death. 24 But God raised Him up again, putting an end to the agony of death, since it was impossible for Him to be held in its power." *See also Acts 26:19-29.*

Scientific Facts

We also know the Bible is true because it contains many scientific facts; facts that the majority of the world did not believe at the time they were written. For example, the earth is round, not flat, as recorded in Isaiah 40:22. "It is He who sits above *the circle of the earth...*"

• Greek mythology taught Atlas held the earth. However, this is what we read in Job 26:7, "He stretches out the north over empty space. And hangs the earth on nothing."

• Matthew Maury, the founder of the science of oceanography, credited the Bible for his finding that the oceans have currents. He cited Psalm 8:8 which includes "... the paths of the seas."

• The Bible talks about the water cycle long before scientific discoveries suggested one exists in the following references.

Ecclesiastes 1:7 "All the rivers flow into the sea, Yet the sea is not full. To the place where the rivers flow, There they flow again."

Amos 9:6 "The One who builds His upper chambers in the heavens And has founded His vaulted dome over the earth, He who calls for the waters of the sea. And pours them out on the face of the earth, The Lord is His name."

> Greek mythology taught Atlas held the earth. However, this is what we read in Job 26:7, "He stretches out the north over empty space. And hangs the earth on nothing."

For many more scientific facts of the Bible, I recommend reading *Scientific Facts in the Bible* by Ray Comfort.

Historical Prophecies

This miraculous Bible contains prophecies written long before they were fulfilled and Daniel 11:2-4 provides an excellent example. Here is what Daniel recorded in 535 BC.

"And now I will tell you the truth. Behold, three more kings are going to arise in Persia. Then a fourth will gain far more riches than all of them; as soon as he becomes strong through his riches, he will arouse the whole empire against the realm of Greece. [3]And a mighty king will arise, and he will rule with great authority and do as he pleases. [4]But as soon as he has arisen, his kingdom will be broken up and parceled out toward the four points of the compass, though not to his own descendants, nor according to his authority which he wielded, for his sovereignty will be uprooted and given to others besides them."

Alright, so what happened? Indeed, there were four kings just as predicted. The first king, Ahasuerus, is known as Cambyses, and he reigned from 530 to 522 B.C. The second king, Pseudo-Smerdis, reigned in 522 B.C. The third king, Darius Hystaspes, reigned from 522 to 486 B.C. And finally, as predicted, the fourth king was wealthy: Xerxes, the son of Darius Hystaspes, who reigned from 486 to 465 B.C. His wealth enabled him to build up vast armies and send them out well supplied.

Xerxes stirred up the Persians against Greece, and in 480 B.C., he invaded Greece with a vast army and navy. However, he was defeated, and that began the decline of the Persian Empire. Alexander the Great comes on the scene in 336 B.C., 200 years after the prophecy was given, and quickly builds a vast empire. What does verse 4 say again? [4]But as soon as he has arisen, his kingdom will be broken up and parceled out toward the four points of the compass, though not to his own descendants, nor according to his authority which he wielded, for his sovereignty will be uprooted and given to others besides them."

What happened with Alexander the Great? He got sick and died, and his family fought over control of the empire, and they all died. The empire was divided among his four generals, not family members, just as predicted.[22] That is amazing! It is so incredible to see God's Word come alive in history.

Daniel 11 predicted the rise and fall of Alexander the Great 200 years before he came on the scene.

Consider the following text:

Who has believed our report?

And to whom has the arm of the LORD been revealed? For He shall grow up before Him as a tender plant, And as a root out of dry ground.

He has no form or comeliness; And when we see Him,

There is no beauty that we should desire Him. He is despised and rejected by men,

A Man of sorrows and acquainted with grief. And we hid, as it were, *our* faces from Him; He was despised, and we did not esteem Him.

Surely He has borne our griefs And carried our sorrows;

Yet we esteemed Him stricken, Smitten by God, and afflicted.

But He *was* wounded for our transgressions,

He was bruised for our iniquities;

The chastisement for our peace *was* upon Him, And by His stripes we are healed.

All we like sheep have gone astray;

We have turned, every one, to his own way;

And the LORD has laid on Him the iniquity of us all. He was oppressed and He was afflicted,

Yet He opened not His mouth;

He was led as a lamb to the slaughter,

And as a sheep before its shearers is silent, So He opened not His mouth.

He was taken from prison and from judgment, And who will declare His generation?

For He was cut off from the land of the living;

For the transgressions of My people He was stricken. And they made His grave with the wicked—

But with the rich at His death, Because He had done no violence, Nor *was any* deceit in His mouth.

Yet it pleased the LORD to bruise Him; He has put *Him* to grief.

When You make His soul an offering for sin,

He shall see *His* seed, He shall prolong *His* days,

And the pleasure of the LORD shall prosper in His hand. He shall see the labor of His soul, *and* be satisfied.

By His knowledge My righteous Servant shall justify many, For He shall bear their iniquities.

Therefore I will divide Him a portion with the great,

And He shall divide the spoil with the strong, Because He poured out His soul unto death, And He was numbered with the transgressors, And He bore the sin of many,

And made intercession for the transgressors.

Who do you suppose is the subject of this text? Think about it. If you guessed, Jesus, you would be correct. What is the source of this text? This text is chapter 53 of the book Isaiah. I removed all headings and verse notations so that it would not be obvious. Now here is the kicker, Isaiah was written about 700 years before the birth of Jesus.

How do we know the Bible is the truth? Let's review the three points we discussed that demonstrate the Bible is truth.

• The writers of the New Testament wrote as eyewitnesses or recorded eyewitness accounts. The events recorded were presented in front of hostile witnesses.

• The Bible contains many scientific facts written down before their scientific discovery.

• The Bible contains many historical prophecies that have come true.

Contradictions in the Bible?

Many people claim they cannot trust the Bible because it has contradictions. Let us look at some examples of scriptures that people cite as being contradictory. We will start at the beginning, in Genesis.

Claim 1: Genesis 1:25-27 shows man was created after the other animals, but Genesis 2:18-19 shows man was created before the other animals. Let us look at both scriptures.

Genesis 1:25-27   ²⁵"God made the beasts of the earth after their kind, and the cattle after their kind, and everything that creeps on the ground after its kind; and God saw that it was good. ²⁶Then God said, 'Let Us make man in Our image, according to Our likeness; and let them rule over the fish of the sea and over the birds of the sky and over the cattle and over all the earth, and over every creeping thing that creeps on the earth.' ²⁷God created man in His own image, in the image of God He created him; male and female He created them."

Genesis 2:18-19   ¹⁸"Then the Lord God said, 'It is not good for the man to be alone; I will make him a helper suitable for him.' ¹⁹Out of the ground the Lord God formed every beast of the field and every bird of the sky, and brought *them* to the man to see what he would call them; and whatever the man called a living creature, that was its name."

Rebuttal to Claim 1: People use scriptures like these and other examples below, to point to contradictions in scriptures. Are these contradictory scriptures? When these scriptures are pulled out of the context they belong in, such as I have done here, they certainly seem to be contradictory. However, to understand the meaning of these scriptures, you must read them in context.

If you read the whole first chapter of Genesis, you will see Genesis 1:25-27, was the end of the summary of creation. In Genesis 2:18-19, we see a detailed account of God planting the Garden of Eden and putting Adam inside it. Inside the Garden of Eden, God makes one of each kind of animal to appear before Adam. When God does this, Adam can see a sample of all the animals that were created, and Adam can see that he is unique. It is after God reveals this fact to Adam that he put Adam to sleep and created Eve from Adam's side. So, these scriptures are not in contradiction.

Claim 2: Scriptures like Proverbs 15:3 and Psalm 139:7-10 illustrate God is everywhere present, sees and knows all things. We can see these attributes of God in many other scriptures as well. Yet Genesis 3:8 and Genesis 18:20-21 seem to show God is not everywhere present, neither sees nor knows all things.

Proverbs 15:3 "The eyes of the Lord are in every place, Watching the evil and the good."

Psalm 139:7-10 [7]"Where can I go from Your Spirit? Or where can I flee from Your presence? [8]If I ascend to heaven, You are there; If I make my bed in Sheol, behold, You are there. [9]If I take the wings of the dawn, If I dwell in the remotest part of the sea, [10]Even there Your hand will lead me, And Your right hand will lay hold of me."

Genesis 3:8 "They heard the sound of the Lord God walking in the garden in the cool of the day, and the man and his wife hid themselves from the presence of the Lord God among the trees of the garden."

Genesis 18:20-21 [20]"And the Lord said, 'The outcry of Sodom and Gomorrah is indeed great, and their sin is exceedingly grave. [21]I will go down now, and see if they have done entirely according to its outcry, which has come to Me; and if not, I will know.'"

In the scriptures from Psalms and Proverbs, it is clear God is everywhere. However, in the Genesis references, we see an account of God in human form asking questions. How can all these accounts be accurate?

Rebuttal to Claim 2: Jesus is the answer. What I mean by that is God the Son, the pre-incarnate Christ, is the Lord. If you read all of Genesis 18, you will see the Lord is walking with two angels and sends them on to Sodom. In both Genesis 3 and 18, the Lord is asking questions to be relational. Think of a parent asking a child about an event. The parent already has all the details of this event, so why ask the question? The answer is obvious. The parent wants to relate to the child. When Abraham observes them going to Sodom to investigate, it is for Abraham's benefit so that Abraham knows the Lord knows just how bad it is.

> Just as a parent wants to relate to the child, God wants to relate to us.

Claim 3: Genesis 8:22 states seedtime and harvest were never to cease. Yet, Genesis 41:54-56 show seedtime and harvest did cease for seven years.

Genesis 8:22 "While the earth remains, Seedtime and harvest, Cold and heat, Winter and summer, And day and night Shall not cease."

Genesis 41:54-56   54"and the seven years of famine began to come, just as Joseph had said, then there was famine in all the lands, but in all the land of Egypt there was bread. 55So when all the land of Egypt was famished, the people cried out to Pharaoh for bread; and Pharaoh said to all the Egyptians, "Go to Joseph; whatever he says to you, you shall do." 56When the famine was *spread* over all the face of the earth, then Joseph opened all the storehouses, and sold to the Egyptians; and the famine was severe in the land of Egypt."

In Genesis 8, we see that seedtime and harvest will not cease. Yet, in Genesis 41, we see that there was no harvest for seven years. Are these contradictory scriptures?

Rebuttal to Claim 3: As I write this, we know that the story referred to in Genesis 41 took place thousands of years ago, yet here we are. What is my point? My point is seedtime and harvest did not cease, or we would not be here today. A seven-year drought is terrible but clearly does not mean seedtime and harvest ceased to occur.

Claim 4: Scriptures James 1:17 and Malachi 3:6 teach God is unchangeable. However, Jonah 3:10 and 1 Samuel 2:30 show God did change.

James 1:17 "Every good thing given and every perfect gift is from above, coming down from the Father of lights, with whom there is no variation or shifting shadow."

Malachi 3:6 "For I, the Lord, do not change; therefore you, O sons of Jacob, are not consumed."

Jonah 3:10 "When God saw their deeds, that they turned from their wicked way, then God relented concerning the calamity which He had declared He would bring upon them. And He did not do *it*."

1 Samuel 2:30 "Therefore the Lord God of Israel declares, 'I did indeed say that your house and the house of your father should walk before Me forever'; but now the Lord declares, 'Far be it from Me—for those who honor Me I will honor, and those who despise Me will be lightly esteemed.'"

Rebuttal to Claim 4: The scriptures from James and Malachi show us God's character and teach us His character is unchanging. The scriptures from Jonah and 1 Samuel do not contradict this. However, what they do reveal is that if we repent, God will show us mercy. Likewise, God is righteous, so if we despise God, we should not expect His mercy. God always was and always will be a righteous judge who can show mercy. His character does not change.

> God always was and always will be a righteous judge who can show mercy. His character does not change.

Claim 5: Deuteronomy 6:4 shows us there is one God, but Genesis 1:26 and Genesis 3:22 clearly speak of a plurality of gods.

Deuteronomy 6:4 "Hear, O Israel! The Lord is our God, the Lord is one!"

Genesis 1:26 "Then God said, 'Let Us make man in Our image, according to Our likeness;'"

Genesis 3:22 "Then the Lord God said, "Behold, the man has become like one of Us, knowing good and evil;"

Rebuttal to Claim 5: There is but one God as declared in Deuteronomy, but the "Us" referred to in Genesis is merely pointing to the fact that He is three-in-one: the Father, Son, and Holy Spirit. Jesus is speaking in John 10:30, and He says, "I and the Father are one." This verse illustrates that there is one God, and Jesus and the Father are one and the same. Jesus also equates the Holy Spirit with the Father and Son when he says to baptize, "in the name of the Father and the Son and the Holy Spirit," in Matthew 28:19.

Claim 6: The passage in 2 Samuel 6:23 teaches Michal had no child; yet, 2 Samuel 21:8 states she had five children.

2 Samuel 6:23 "Michal the daughter of Saul had no child to the day of her death."

2 Samuel 21:8 "So the king took Armoni and Mephibosheth, the two sons of Rizpah the daughter of Aiah, whom she bore to Saul, and the five sons of Michal the daughter of Saul, whom she brought up for Adriel the son of Barzillai the Meholathite." (KJV)

Rebuttal for Claim 6: If you read 2 Samuel 21:8 carefully, you see that the five sons of Michal are children she brought up for Adriel. Chapter 6 is letting us know she did not give birth to any children, and chapter 21 shows us she did raise five sons.

Claim 7: Second Samuel 24:9 tells us the number of fighting men of Israel was 800,000; and of Judah 500,000. Yet, 1 Chronicles 21:5 reveals the number of fighting men of Israel was 1,100,000; and of Judah 470,000.

2 Samuel 24:9 "And Joab gave the number of the registration of the people to the king; and there were in Israel eight hundred thousand valiant men who drew the sword, and the men of Judah were five hundred thousand men."

1 Chronicles 21:5 "Joab gave the number of the census of *all* the people to David. And all Israel were 1,100,000 men who drew the sword; and Judah *was* 470,000 men who drew the sword."

Rebuttal to Claim 7: If you read 2 Samuel carefully, you will see it tells us the number of valiant men in Israel, and 1 Chronicles shows us all the men who drew the sword in Israel totaled one million one hundred thousand men. The critical difference is the word "valiant." Then in 2 Samuel, it refers to the men of Judah were five hundred thousand, yet in 1 Chronicles it says, "four hundred and seventy thousand men who drew the sword."

What we see are two different accounts that emphasize different details. Consider this analogy. If there were a court case with witnesses testifying to some event, and all the witnesses shared the exact same story with the exact same details, then you might suspect collusion between the witnesses and the testimonies might possibly be thrown out. What we have here in Scripture are two different accounts of the same story with *different* details, not *contradictory* details. In reality, the different details validates the Scripture's accuracy even more.

Claim 8: Matthew 5:1-3 reveals Christ preached his first sermon, "The Beatitudes" on the mount. Luke 6:17-20 illustrates Christ preached his first sermon, "The Beatitudes," on the plain.

Matthew 5:1-3 "When Jesus saw the crowds, He went up on the mountain; and after He sat down, His disciples came to Him. ² He opened His mouth and *began* to teach them, saying, ³ "Blessed are the poor in spirit, for theirs is the kingdom of heaven."

 Luke 6:17-20 ¹⁷"Jesus came down with them and stood on a level place; and *there was* a large crowd of His disciples, and a great throng of people from all Judea and Jerusalem and the coastal region of Tyre and Sidon, ¹⁸ who had come to hear Him and to be healed of their diseases; and those who were troubled with unclean spirits were being cured. ¹⁹ And all the people were trying to touch Him, for power was coming from Him and healing *them* all. ²⁰ And turning His gaze toward His disciples, He *began* to say, "Blessed *are* you *who are* poor, for yours is the kingdom of God."

Rebuttal to Claim 8: Jesus did not have the advantage of modern radio or TV. If he wanted his message heard by multiple groups of people, he would have to give the message to each group. Matthew and Luke are recording the same message but given at different times and places.

Claim 9: Mark 15:25 tells us Christ was crucified *at the third hour*. Yet John 19:14-15 reveals Christ was not crucified until *after the sixth hour*.

Mark 15:25 "It was the third hour when they crucified Him."

John 19:14-15 "Now it was the day of preparation for the Passover; it was about the sixth hour. And he said to the Jews,

"Behold, your King!" **15** So they cried out, "Away with *Him*, away with *Him*, crucify Him!" Pilate *said to them, "Shall I crucify your King?" The chief priests answered, "We have no king but Caesar."

Rebuttal to Claim 9: Most of the claims of contradiction can be easily rectified by simply carefully reading the text, and studying the context. This one is different. This one requires additional research to understand the times given by Mark and John, and thus, understanding each author's audience.

Mark was writing to a Jewish audience. To the Jew of this period, the day started at 6:00 AM. Therefore, when Mark wrote, "It was the third hour when they crucified Him", it would be correct to translate this using the modern time of 9:00 AM. On the other hand, John's audience was mostly non-Jewish, and he would have used the Roman time that is still in use today with the day starting at midnight. Therefore, John's reference to the "sixth hour" is a reference to 6:00 AM.[23] Therefore, it is in agreement with the Mark passage because Jesus was crucified *after* 6:00 AM.

Claim 10: Matthew 27:44 informs us that the two thieves crucified with Christ reviled Christ, but Luke 23:39-40 shows that only one of the thieves reviled Christ.

Matthew 27:44 "The robbers who had been crucified with Him were also insulting Him with the same words."

Luke 23:39-40 "One of the criminals who were hanged *there* was hurling abuse at Him, saying, "Are You not the Christ? Save Yourself and us!" **40** But the other answered, and rebuking him said, "Do you not even fear God, since you are under the same sentence of condemnation?"

Rebuttal for Claim 10: Have you ever gone along with some buddies in teasing a person? Then, one of your buddies carries the teasing too far, and you stop and say enough? We see similar chiding happening here. Both criminals revile Christ as recorded by Matthew, but one of them takes it too far, and the other one comes to Jesus' defense.

Claim 11: Matthew 27:5 tells us Judas returned the money and hung himself, but Acts 1:18 suggests he bought a field and died another way.

Matthew 27:5 "And he threw the pieces of silver into the temple sanctuary and departed; and he went away and hanged himself."

Acts 1:18 "Now this man acquired a field with the price of his wickedness, and falling headlong, he burst open in the middle and all his intestines gushed out."

Rebuttal for Claim 11: Matthew and Acts show us two different sets of details about the same event. Matthew records two facts: Judas threw the money into the temple, and Judas hung himself. Of course, those that had a role in giving the money to Judas did not want anything to do with the returned money. So, the wicked chief priests used the money to purchase a field in which to bury strangers, criminals, and the poor and attributed it to Judas.

This is also what we see in Acts. Acts reveals some additional details of what happened after Judas' death. Judas likely hung himself by tying a rope to a tree branch. Then, after some time, either the rope or the tree branch broke, and Judas fell. His intestines gushed out of his decomposing body when it hit the rocks below. Going back to a court case analogy, different details by different witnesses is what we would expect.

Claim 12: Mark 3:29 teaches there is an unpardonable sin. However, Acts 13:39 suggests there is not.

Mark 3:29 "but whoever blasphemes against the Holy Spirit never has forgiveness, but is guilty of an eternal sin"

Acts 13:39 "and through Him everyone who believes is freed from all things, from which you could not be freed through the Law of Moses."

Rebuttal for Claim 12: When Mark says, "whoever blasphemes against the Holy Spirit never has forgiveness," he means that anyone who rejects Jesus has no forgiveness. Obviously, you have not followed what it says in Acts, "everyone who believes is freed from all things" if you rejected Jesus. See, you must believe in Jesus Christ to be justified. If you do not believe, there is no forgiveness of sins. These scriptures in Mark and Acts are in harmony with one another, not contrary.

These claims of contradiction are shared to show that there are no contradictions in the Bible. Now, you may come across other claims, but these are included so that with careful examination of the scriptures, you can see the claim of contradictions disappears.

Summary on the Bible's Authenticity

In this chapter on the Bible, we looked at characteristics of the Bible, such as there are 66 books recorded by many human writers, inspired by one God. We discovered that we can trust the Scriptures that were handed down from one generation to another because the scribes used unparalleled detail in making copies, even noting things like the number of times each letter of the alphabet occurred in each book and compared it to the original.

We saw that the information contained in the Bible can be trusted as God's Word. We examined scientific facts recorded in the Bible long before man discovered them. We saw examples of historical prophecies such as the reference to Alexander the Great and how the prophecy came true. Finally, we looked at many claims of contradiction between scriptures and why those claims are not valid. *We can absolutely know the Bible is the True Word of God and trust it as our ultimate authority.*

Who Is God?

Chapter 4

Now that we can see the Bible is the inspired, infallible Word of God, let us answer some questions about who God is. The following scriptures do not need any explanation for a person to understand them. Just read them.

Is God Really All Knowing?

Job 37:14-16 – [14]"Listen to this, O Job, Stand and consider the wonders of God. [15] "Do you know how God establishes them, And makes the lightning of His cloud to shine? [16] Do you know about the layers of the thick clouds, The wonders of one perfect in knowledge,"

Psalm 147:4-5 [4] "He counts the number of the stars; He gives names to all of them. [5] Great is our Lord and abundant in strength; His understanding is infinite."

1 Samuel 2:3 "Boast no more so very proudly, Do not let arrogance come out of your mouth; For the Lord is a God of knowledge, And with Him actions are weighed."

Isaiah 55:8-9 [8]"For My thoughts are not your thoughts, Nor are your ways My ways," declares the Lord. [9]"For as the heavens are higher than the earth, So are My ways higher than your ways and My thoughts than your thoughts."

1 John 3:19-20 [19] "We will know by this that we are of the truth, and will assure our heart before Him in whatever our heart condemns us; [20] for God is greater than our heart and knows all things.

Hebrews 4:13 "And there is no creature hidden from His sight, but all things are open and laid bare to the eyes of Him with whom we have to do."

Isaiah 46:10 "Declaring the end from the beginning, And from ancient times things which have not been done, Saying, 'My purpose will be established, And I will accomplish all My good pleasure';"

Matthew 10:29-30 [29]"Are not two sparrows sold for a cent? And yet not one of them will fall to the ground apart from your Father. [30]But the very hairs of your head are all numbered."

Psalm 139:3-4 [3]"You scrutinize my path and my lying down, And are intimately acquainted with all my ways. [4]Even before there is a word on my tongue, Behold, O Lord, You know it all."

> Psalm 139:3 "You scrutinize my path and my lying down, And are intimately acquainted with all my ways.

The above scriptures reveal the omniscience (all-knowing) attribute of God. Now let's take a look at another attribute of almighty God.

Is God Really All Powerful?

Genesis 1:1-3 ¹"In the beginning God created the heavens and the earth. ²The earth was formless and void, and darkness was over the surface of the deep, and the Spirit of God was moving over the surface of the waters. ³Then God said, "Let there be light"; and there was light."

Jeremiah 32:27 "Behold, I am the Lord, the God of all flesh; is anything too difficult for Me?"

Psalm 66:5-7 ⁵"Come and see the works of God, *Who is* awesome in *His* deeds toward the sons of men. ⁶He turned the sea into dry land; They passed through the river on foot; There let us rejoice in Him! ⁷He rules by His might forever; His eyes keep watch on the nations; Let not the rebellious exalt themselves."

Job 42:2 "I know that You can do all things, And that no purpose of Yours can be thwarted."

Isaiah 40:28 "Do you not know? Have you not heard? The Everlasting God, the Lord, the Creator of the ends of the earth does not become weary or tired. His understanding is inscrutable."

Psalm 33:9 "For He spoke, and it was done; He commanded, and it stood fast."

Matthew 19:26 "And looking at them Jesus said to them, 'With people this is impossible, but with God all things are possible.'"

Colossians 1:16-17 ¹⁶"For by Him all things were created, both in the heavens and on earth, visible and invisible, whether thrones or dominions or rulers or authorities—all things have been created through Him and for Him. [17]He is before all things, and in Him all things hold together."

Hebrews 1:3 "And He is the radiance of His glory and the exact representation of His nature, and upholds all things by the word of His power. When He had made purification of sins, He sat down at the right hand of the Majesty on high,"

In the above scriptures, we see that nothing is impossible for God. He is omnipotent. Now let us take a look at one more attribute.

Is God Really Everywhere?

1 Kings 8:27 "But will God indeed dwell on the earth? Behold, heaven and the highest heaven cannot contain You, how much less this house which I have built!"

Psalm 139:7-10 [7]"Where can I go from Your Spirit? Or where can I flee from Your presence? [8]If I ascend to heaven, You are there; If I make my bed in Sheol, behold, You are there. [9]If I take the wings of the dawn, If I dwell in the remotest part of the sea, [10]Even there Your hand will lead me, And Your right hand will lay hold of me."

Proverbs 15:3 "The eyes of the Lord are in every place, watching the evil and the good."

Jeremiah 23:23-24 [23]"Can a man hide himself in hiding places So I do not see him?" declares the Lord. [24]"Do I not fill the heavens and the earth?" declares the Lord.

> Proverbs 15:3 "The eyes of the Lord are in every place, watching the evil and the good."

When sharing these scriptures, I have heard the question asked, "If God is all-knowing, and can do all things, then can God make a rock so big He can't pick it up?"

Now, is this a logical question?

No, not really. You cannot compare an infinite God with a finite object. No matter how big the rock is, it still has a finite size. The question also shows a lack of understanding of God's nature. If the point of the question is that there are things God cannot do, then I say, "Of course there are things God cannot do." You see, His omnipotence is not something independent of His nature. It is part of His nature. God has a nature, and His attributes operate within that nature.

What do I mean? Well, for example, God is truth; therefore, He cannot lie. God loves you and cannot hate you. He is bound only by His nature, which is perfect.

Another question that often is asked is this one, "If God is all-powerful, and everywhere, then why does evil exist?"

The answer is relatively simple. Evil exists because God loves us and desires a relationship with us. Therefore, God did not design mind-numb robots. God wants us to *choose* Him, so He must give us the freedom not to choose Him. Because we have a choice, God allowed for the possibility of evil. Evil exists because people have chosen to disobey God.

Every single one of us has chosen to disobey God at some point. (See 1 John 2:1-5). If you have told one lie (and we all have), you are a liar and have broken God's law. We have not just broken God's law, we have utterly disregarded it. We have tossed it aside along with all of God's principles and even declared there is no

God. The question should not be, "Why is there evil?", but rather, "How could a holy, just God love sinners?" We should be thankful for God's goodness and forgiveness, for the fact that God has not completely abandoned us, but instead has provided us the way of redemption according to His never-ending love.

Who Is Jesus?

Chapter 5

No matter what you think of Jesus, no historical figure has had a more significant impact on the history of the world than Jesus of Nazareth. So, who is Jesus? First, we will look at what some outside of Christianity say about Jesus.

According to the Muslims

Muslims teach Jesus was a messenger of God.

"The Messiah (Jesus), son of Mary, was no more than a Messenger before whom many Messengers have passed away; and his mother adhered wholly to truthfulness, and they both ate food (as other mortals do). See how We make Our signs clear to them; and see where they are turning away!" (Quran 5:75)

The Bible clearly teaches he was much more than a messenger, but more on that later.

Muslims teach he was born of a Virgin Mother.

"Relate in the Book the story of Mary, when she withdrew from her family, to a place in the East. She screened herself from them; then We sent to her Our spirit (angel Gabriel) and he appeared before her as a man in all respects. She said: I seek refuge from you in God Most Gracious (come not near) if you do fear God. He said: Nay, I am only a Messenger from your Lord, to announce to you the gift of a pure son. She said: How shall I have a son, when no man has ever touched me, and I am not unchaste? He said: So it will be, your Lord says: 'That is easy for Me; and We wish to appoint him as a sign unto men and a Mercy from Us': It was a matter so decreed" (Quran 19:16-21).

Muslims teach Jesus performed miracles.

"Then will God say: 'O Jesus the son of Mary! recount My favor to you and to your mother. Behold! I strengthened you with the Holy Spirit (the angel Gabriel) so that you did speak to the people in childhood and in maturity. Behold! I taught you the Book and Wisdom, the Law and the Gospel. And behold: you make out of clay, as it were, the figure of a bird, by My leave, and you breathe into it, and it becomes a bird by My leave, and you heal those born blind, and the lepers by My leave. And behold! you bring forth the dead by My leave. And behold! I did restrain the children of Israel from (violence to you) when you did show them the Clear Signs, and the unbelievers among them said: 'This is nothing but evident magic' (Quran 5:110).

It is interesting that the Muslims believe Mary was a virgin when she conceived Jesus, and they believe Jesus performed miracles, yet they see Jesus as just a messenger.

Muslims teach that Jesus was not the son of God.

"Say: "God is Unique! God, the Source [of everything]. He has not fathered anyone nor was He fathered, and there is nothing comparable to Him!" (Quran 112:1-4). "Such was Jesus, the son of Mary; it is a statement of truth, about which they vainly dispute.

It is not befitting to the majesty of God, that He should beget a son. Glory be to Him! When He determines a matter, He only says to it, 'Be' and it is" (Quran 19:34-35).

This passage from the Quran is *not* what the Bible teaches. The following verses from Scripture tell us unequivocally that Jesus was the Son of God.

Biblical Teaching

John 3:16 "For God so loved the world, that He gave His only begotten Son, that whoever believes in Him shall not perish, but have eternal life."

John 1:1-3 [1]In the beginning was the Word, and the Word was with God, and the Word was God. [2]He was in the beginning with God. [3]All things came into being through Him, and apart from Him nothing came into being that has come into being."

These two scriptures show us not only Jesus is the Son of God, He was always with God, and everything was created through Jesus.

Muslims teach Jesus was hung on a cross, but not to the point of death.

"They did not kill him, nor did they crucify him, but they thought they did. God lifted him up to His presence. God is Almighty, All-Wise" (Quran 4:156-157).

Muslims teach Jesus never died, and was never buried; but that God took Him to heaven before He could die.

This belief is also not what the Bible teaches. However, there are some outside of the Muslim religion and other world religions, who believe Jesus did not die on the cross. From my studies, I find only Muslims believe Jesus simply vanished from the cross and was taken to heaven before death. Others believe Jesus was taken off the cross before dying and placed in a tomb where he then revived in the cool of the tomb.

Neither of these options makes sense. First, Jesus was not going to disappear to heaven without dying because that defeats God's plan of salvation which existed from the beginning. Read Isaiah 53.

Second, it is not logical to think Jesus was not dead when the Roman soldiers took him down from the cross. Jesus was beaten almost to the point of death before he was nailed to the cross. The Roman soldiers knew their job, and they did it well. They were abundantly acquainted with death, and they were not going to do their job part way. To verify Jesus was dead, before they took him down one of the soldiers stabbed Jesus in the side. Due to the severe whipping Jesus received prior to the cross, and then the hanging on the cross, he would have experienced a hypovolemic shock. This shock would cause rapid heartbeat, then fluid would gather in the area around the heart. This is called pericardial effusion. Therefore, when Jesus was stabbed, fluid came out along with blood.[24] That is precisely what John records in John 19.

John 19:31-34   [31]"Then the Jews, because it was the day of preparation, so that the bodies would not remain on the cross on the Sabbath (for that Sabbath was a high day), asked Pilate that their legs might be broken, and *that* they might be taken away. [32]So the soldiers came, and broke the legs of the first man and of the other who was crucified with Him; [33]but coming to Jesus, when they saw that He was already dead, they did not break His legs. [34]But one of the soldiers pierced His side with a spear, and immediately blood and water came out."

So, there is no doubt Jesus was dead, dead, dead, dead, dead, dead.

According to the Mormons

Unlike the Muslims, the Mormons strive to *appear the same as* Christians and give statements regarding Jesus much the same as a Christian would. They even use Bible verses when doing so. The problem is, they redefine the terms the Christian would use to match their own beliefs.

When anyone redefines who Jesus is and what he did, they have a different Christ — a false Christ. For example, if I were to teach that, "Jesus was born in Japan in 1820; He killed 24 people; He lied to many people during his lifetime; And He finally died in 1902 of old age," I would not be teaching about the Jesus of the Bible.

So, what *do* Mormons believe? We will use standard Mormon books to look at some teachings of the Mormon Church.

> When anyone redefines who Jesus is and what he did, they have a different Christ — a false Christ

Mormons teach God was once a mortal man

God was once a mortal man. He lived on a planet like our own. He experienced conditions similar to our own and advanced step by step. (*Achieving Celestial Marriage Manual*, abbreviated ACCM, p.129).

Late LDS apostle Bruce R. McConkie wrote [quoting Joseph Smith]: "Further, as the Prophet also taught, there is a god above the father of our Lord Jesus Christ...If Jesus Christ was the son of God, and John discovered that God the Father of Jesus Christ had a father also...Was there ever a son without a father?" (*Mormon Doctrine*, abbreviated MD, p.322).

God is now an exalted man with powers of eternal increase. He lives in an exalted Marriage relationship (ACMM, p.129).

Now let us compare this Mormon teaching with scripture from the Bible.

Biblical Teaching

Isaiah 43:10 "You are My witnesses," declares the Lord, "And My servant whom I have chosen, So that you may know and believe Me and understand that I am He. Before Me there was no God formed, and there will be none after Me."

Isaiah 44:6-8   6"Thus says the Lord, the King of Israel and his Redeemer, the Lord of hosts: 'I am the first and I am the last, And there is no God besides Me.   7Who is like Me? Let him proclaim and declare it; Yes, let him recount it to Me in order, from the time that I established the ancient nation. And let them declare to them the things that are coming And the events that are going to take place.   8Do not tremble and do not be afraid; Have I not long since announced *it* to you and declared *it*? And you are My witnesses. Is there any God besides Me, Or is there any *other* Rock? I know of none.'"

John 1:1-4   1"In the beginning was the Word, and the Word was with God, and the Word was God.   2He was in the beginning with God.   3All things came into being through Him, and apart from Him nothing came into being that has come into being.   4In Him was life, and the life was the Light of men."

Revelation 22:13   "I am the Alpha and the Omega, the first and the last, the beginning and the end."

John 17:3 "This is eternal life, that they may know You, the only true God, and Jesus Christ whom You have sent."

> Isaiah 44:6 "Thus says the Lord, the King of Israel and his Redeemer, the Lord of hosts: 'I am the first and I am the last, And there is no God besides Me.

So, the Mormons teach an endless cycle of men becoming gods, and God the Father was once a human son. However, the Bible teaches that God is the beginning and the end, and there are no other gods.

Mormons teach Jesus provides immortality for all people regardless of their faith

"Jesus is the only person on earth to be born of a mortal mother and an immortal father. That is why he is called the Only Begotten Son" (*Gospel Principles* [GP], p. 64). His atonement (death and resurrection) provides immortality for all people regardless of their faith. "Christ thus overcame physical death. Because of his atonement, everyone born on this earth will be resurrected . . . This condition is called immortality. All people who ever lived will be resurrected, 'both old and young, both bond and free, both male and female, both the wicked and the righteous'" (*The Book of Mormon* [BOM], Alma 11:44)" (*GP*, p. 74).

Now let's see what the Bible says on this.

Biblical Teaching

John 3:36 "He who believes in the Son has everlasting life, and he who does not believe the Son shall not see life, but the wrath of God abides on him."

Revelation 21:8 "But for the cowardly and unbelieving and abominable and murderers and immoral persons and sorcerers and idolaters and all liars, their part *will be* in the lake that burns with fire and brimstone, which is the second death."

Salvation is a free gift we can have, but only if we choose to accept it. We can choose to reject the gift, and if we reject His gift, we will not have the righteousness of God in us. Romans 6:23 tells us, "For the wages of sin is death..." Therefore, we can be sure that all do not have atonement regardless of their faith.

Mormons teach God the Father has a body of flesh and bones

"The Father has a body of flesh and bones as tangible as man's; the Son also; but the Holy Ghost has not a body of flesh and bones, but is a personage of Spirit. Were it not so, the Holy Ghost could not dwell in us" (Doctrine & Covenants 130:22).

Now compare that passage with this one from the Gospel of John.

John 4:24 "God is spirit, and those who worship Him must worship in spirit and truth."

Mormons teach everyone born on earth was a spirit brother or sister in heaven

"Every person who was ever born on earth was our spirit brother or sister in heaven. The first spirit born to our heavenly parents was Jesus Christ, so he is literally our elder brother" (GP, p. 11).

Scripture tells us we are not a child of God until we are adopted into His family by trusting Jesus.

Biblical Teaching

Romans 8:14-16   [14]"For all who are being led by the Spirit of God, these are sons of God. [15]For you have not received a spirit of slavery leading to fear again, but you have received a spirit of adoption as sons by which we cry out, 'Abba! Father!' [16]The Spirit Himself testifies with our spirit that we are children of God,"

John 1:10-18   [10]"He was in the world, and the world was made through Him, and the world did not know Him. [11]He came to His own, and those who were His own did not receive Him. [12]But as many as received Him, to them He gave the right to become children of God, *even* to those who believe in His name, [13]who were born, not of blood nor of the will of the flesh nor of the will of man, but of God. [14]And the Word became flesh, and dwelt among us, and we saw His glory, glory as of the only begotten from the Father, full of grace and truth. [15]John *testified about Him and cried out, saying, "This was He of whom I said, 'He who comes after me has a higher rank than I, for He existed before me.'" [16]For of His fullness we have all received, and grace upon grace. [17]For the Law was given through Moses; grace and truth were realized through Jesus Christ. [18]No one has seen God at any time; the only begotten God who is in the bosom of the Father, He has explained *Him*.

Mormons teach Jesus and Lucifer are bothers

"Lucifer, our elder brother who desired the glory for himself, stood up and proposed his own plan" (Moses 4:1-4, Abraham 3:27-28, *Pearl of Great Price*).

"His [Jesus'] trials were continuous. Perhaps his brother, Lucifer, had heard him say when he was still but a lad of 12, 'Whist ye not that I must be about my Father's business?'" (Luke 2:49) "...Then came the time when Satan thought to trip him. Their encounter in the previous world had been on more equal terms, but now Jesus was young and Satan was experienced" (Ensign, official Church magazine, December 1980, pp.3-5. "Jesus of Nazareth," Spencer W. Kimball, First Presidency Message).

"Jesus stood and offered himself as our sin-offering, giving man his free agency and the chance to attain eternal glory, or godhood with heavenly father" (Moses 4:2).

"All the council voted No to Lucifer and Yes to Jesus" (Abraham 3:28).

"Lucifer, very angry, persuaded one-third of the spirit children to follow him and rebel against God and the plan of Jesus. They were cast from God's presence and sent to this earth without bodies of flesh and bone" (Abraham 3:28, D&C 29:36-37).

However, what you will see in the Scripture below is that Lucifer is a created being, as all angels are. Also, in the scripture from Colossians, we see Jesus created everything in heaven, and since Jesus created everything, He created Lucifer. They are not brothers. Ezekiel describes Lucifer in chapter 28.

Biblical Teaching

Ezekiel 28:13-17 [13]"You were in Eden, the garden of God; Every precious stone was your covering: The ruby, the topaz and the diamond; The beryl, the onyx and the jasper; The lapis lazuli, the turquoise and the emerald; And the gold, the workmanship of your settings and sockets, Was in you. On the day that you were created They were prepared. [14]You were the anointed cherub who covers, And I placed you *there*. You were on the holy mountain of God; You walked in the midst of the stones of fire. [15]You were blameless in your ways From the day you were created until unrighteousness was found in you. [16]By the abundance of your trade you were internally filled with violence, And you sinned; Therefore I have cast you as profane from the mountain of God. And I have destroyed you, O covering cherub, from the midst of the stones of fire. [17]Your heart was lifted up because of your beauty; You corrupted your wisdom by reason of your splendor..."

On the other hand, if we take a look at Colossians (as well as other books), we see Jesus created all things.

> ...Lucifer is a created being, as all angels are. Also, in the scripture from Colossians, we see Jesus created everything in heaven, and since Jesus created everything, He created Lucifer.

Colossians 1:13-20 [13]"For He rescued us from the domain of darkness, and transferred us to the kingdom of His beloved Son, [14] in whom we have redemption, the forgiveness of sins. [15]He is the image of the invisible God, the firstborn of all creation. [16]For by Him all things were created, *both* in the heavens and on earth, visible and invisible, whether thrones or dominions or rulers or authorities—all things have been created through Him and for Him. ¹⁷He is before all things, and in Him all things hold together. ¹⁸He is also head of the body, the church; and He is the beginning, the firstborn from the dead, so that He Himself will come to have first place in everything. ¹⁹For it was the *Father's* good pleasure for all the fullness to dwell in Him, ²⁰and through Him to reconcile all things to Himself, having made peace through the blood of His cross; through Him, *I say*, whether things on earth or things in heaven."

So, again, Jesus created Lucifer. Lucifer is an angel, but not just any angel, he is a cherub and the most glamorous of all. He was made more beautiful than all the other angels and became prideful. His pride was his downfall.

While we learned earlier, there are no contradictions in scripture. We see there are many contradictions between what the Mormons teach and the Bible. These are just a few examples, but I shared these examples so that anyone can see the Mormon teaching on Jesus and the Bible's teaching on Jesus are not the same, as Mormons allege.

According to the Jehovah Witnesses

Jehovah's Witnesses are similar to Mormons in that they identify themselves as part of Christianity. We need to look no further than how Jehovah Witnesses view Christ to see that their beliefs are vastly different from what the Bible teaches.

Jehovah Witnesses teach Jesus Christ was Michael the Archangel

Jesus Christ was Michael the Archangel before becoming a man.

"...the Son of God was known as Michael before he came to earth" (Reasoning from the Scriptures, p. 218).

After Jesus died, he was resurrected with His original identity as Michael the Archangel.

"Read carefully the following Bible account: 'War broke out in heaven: Michael [who is the resurrected Jesus Christ] and his angels battled with the dragon'" (You Can Live Forever in Paradise on Earth, 1982, p. 21).

Biblical Teaching

As we already saw in the previous section on Mormons, Jesus created the angels. He was never an angel. However, to illustrate a couple of differences between Michael the archangel and Jesus, we can look at the Bible. We see in Jude 9 that Michael did not rebuke an evil spirit himself, but let the Lord rebuke him.

Jude 9 "But Michael the archangel, when he disputed with the devil and argued about the body of Moses, did not dare pronounce against him a railing judgment, but said, 'The Lord rebuke you!'"

Who is "The Lord" in this passage? Is Michael referring to himself? No, he is referring to Jesus.

So, in Jude 9 we see Michael use Jesus to rebuke an evil spirit. However, in Mark 9 we see Jesus himself commands the spirit:

Mark 9:25 "When Jesus saw that a crowd was rapidly gathering, He rebuked the unclean spirit, saying to it, 'You deaf and mute spirit, I command you, come out of him and do not enter him again.'"

Angels are not given the authority to rule the world.

Hebrews 2:4-5 [4]"God also testifying with them, both by signs and wonders and by various miracles and by gifts of the Holy Spirit according to His own will. [5]For He did not subject to angels the world to come, concerning which we are speaking."

However, Jesus will rule the world.

Luke 1:32-33 [32]"He will be great and will be called the Son of the Most High; and the Lord God will give Him the throne of His father David; [33]and He will reign over the house of Jacob forever, and His kingdom will have no end."

Jehovah Witnesses teach Jesus is not Almighty God

In the New World Translation (NWT) of the Holy Scriptures (The Jehovah Witnesses's bible), John 1:1 says, "In the beginning was the Word. The Word was with God, and the Word was a god." "...that is the Word was a powerful godlike one. Clearly, Jesus is not Almighty God."

Biblical Teaching

What a difference one little word can make. Did you catch it? Again, (NWT) "The Word was with God, and the Word was a god." The Jehovah Witnesses' translation has, "Word was *a god*" instead of "Word *was God*." So, the Jehovah's Witnesses are polytheistic. They see Jesus as a god and not the God, and clearly, they don't see Jesus as Almighty God. However, John 10:30 says, "I and the Father are one." Colossians 1 makes this pretty clear.

Colossians 1:15-17 [15]"He is the image of the invisible God, the firstborn of all creation. [16]For by Him all things were created, *both* in the heavens and on earth, visible and invisible, whether thrones or dominions or rulers or authorities—all things have been created through Him and for Him. ¹⁷He is before all things, and in Him all things hold together."

Both the Mormons and Jehovah Witnesses take the Jesus of the Bible and change him into something other than what the Bible teaches. The Mormons make him the brother of Lucifer. Jehovah's Witnesses make him Michael the archangel. Yet, the Bible is clear. He is one with the Father, creator of everything, King of Kings and Lord of Lords.

According to the Jews

What about the Jews? How do they see Jesus? In general, they believe him to be a good person, but one that did not fulfill Messianic prophecies. They also think he may have been insane.

Mark 3:21 "But when His own people heard about this, they went out to lay hold of Him, for they said, 'He is out of His mind.'"

Mark 3:31-32 ³¹"Then His brothers and His mother came, and standing outside they sent to Him, calling Him. ³²And a multitude was sitting around Him; and they said to Him, 'Look, Your mother and Your brothers are outside seeking You.'"

However, the main reason the Jews do not see Jesus as the Messiah is unfulfilled prophecies, such as bringing about world peace.

Isaiah 2:2-4 ²"Now it will come about that in the last days the mountain of the house of the Lord will be established as the chief of the mountains, And will be raised above the hills; and all the nations will stream to it. ³And many peoples will come and say, 'Come, let us go up to the mountain of the Lord, to the house of the God of Jacob; that He may teach us concerning His ways, and that we may walk in His paths.' For the law will go forth from Zion and the word of the Lord from Jerusalem. ⁴ And He will judge between the nations, and will render decisions for many peoples; and they will hammer their swords into plowshares and their spears into pruning hooks. Nation will not lift up sword against nation, and never again will they learn war."

The Jews may also point to a prophecy like this one in order to justify their rejection of Jesus as the Messiah who did not bring world peace.

Isaiah 11:4-7 ⁴"But with righteousness He will judge the poor, And decide with fairness for the afflicted of the earth; And He will strike the earth with the rod of His mouth, And with the breath of His lips He will slay the wicked. ⁵Also righteousness will be the belt about His loins, And faithfulness the belt about His waist. ⁶And the wolf will dwell with the lamb, And the leopard will lie down with the young goat, And the calf and the young lion and the fatling together; And a little boy will lead them. ⁷Also the cow and the bear will graze, Their young will lie down together, And the lion will eat straw like the ox.

So, the Jewish expectation is that the Messiah will not only bring about world peace between people, but He will also bring peace between all the animals.

Biblical Response to the Jews Rejection of Jesus as Their Messiah

However, what is essential to understand is that Jesus did not fail to fulfill these prophecies. Rather, the time to fulfill them has not yet come. He will fulfill these prophecies when he comes back to set up His earthly kingdom to rule and reign for 1,000 years. The Jews make the mistake of thinking Jesus needed to fulfill all prophecies the first time. However, the first time Jesus came to earth, His purpose was to redeem us spiritually. The next time he comes, He will be the conquering hero the Jews were expecting.

Unfortunately for many, when Jesus comes again, it will be too late to put your trust in Him. Your chance to do that is now.

> Unfortunately for many, when Jesus comes again, it will be too late to put your trust in Him. Your chance to do that is now.

What Does the Old Testament Prophesy about the Messiah?

Chapter 6

So, what does the Old Testament prophecies teach us about Jesus, the Messiah? The Old Testament prophets actually told us hundreds of years ahead of time what we can expect of the Messiah.

The Messiah will be a descendant of David.

Jeremiah 33:15   "In those days and at that time I will cause a righteous Branch of David to spring forth; and He shall execute justice and righteousness on the earth."

How was the prophecy fulfilled?

Luke 1:31-32   [31]"And behold, you will conceive in your womb and bear a son, and you shall name Him Jesus. [32]He will be great and will be called the Son of the Most High; and the Lord God will give Him the throne of His father David."

The Messiah will be born of a virgin.

Isaiah 7:14   "Therefore the Lord Himself will give you a sign: Behold, a virgin will be with child and bear a son, and she will call His name Immanuel."

How was the prophecy fulfilled?

Matthew 1:20-21   **20**"But when he had considered this, behold, an angel of the Lord appeared to him in a dream, saying, "Joseph, son of David, do not be afraid to take Mary as your wife; for the Child who has been conceived in her is of the Holy Spirit. **21**She will bear a Son; and you shall call His name Jesus, for He will save His people from their sins.""

The Messiah will be born in Bethlehem.

Micah 5:2 "But as for you, Bethlehem Ephrathah, *Too* little to be among the clans of Judah, from you One will go forth for Me to be ruler in Israel. His goings forth are from long ago, from the days of eternity."

How was the prophecy fulfilled?

Luke 2:4-7   **4**"Joseph also went up from Galilee, from the city of Nazareth, to Judea, to the city of David which is called Bethlehem, because he was of the house and family of David, **5**in order to register along with Mary, who was engaged to him, and was with child. **6**While they were there, the days were completed for her to give birth. **7**And she gave birth to her firstborn son; and she wrapped Him in cloths, and laid Him in a manger, because there was no room for them in the inn."

Great kings will pay homage and tribute to the Messiah.

Psalm 72:10 "Let the kings of Tarshish and of the islands bring presents; The kings of Sheba and Seba offer gifts."

How was the prophecy fulfilled?

Matthew 2:1-2 [1]"Now after Jesus was born in Bethlehem of Judea in the days of Herod the king, magi from the east arrived in Jerusalem, saying, [2]'Where is He who has been born King of the Jews? For we saw His star in the east and have come to worship Him.'"

A Messenger would precede the Messiah.

Isaiah 40:3 "A voice is calling, 'Clear the way for the Lord in the wilderness; Make smooth in the desert a highway for our God.'"

How was the prophecy fulfilled?

Matthew 3:1-2 [1]"Now in those days John the Baptist came, preaching in the wilderness of Judea, saying, [2]'Repent, for the kingdom of heaven is at hand.'"

The Spirit of the LORD shall rest upon Him.

Isaiah 11:2 "The Spirit of the Lord will rest on Him, The spirit of wisdom and understanding, The spirit of counsel and strength, The spirit of knowledge and the fear of the Lord."

How was the prophecy fulfilled?

Matthew 3:16-17 [16]"After being baptized, Jesus came up immediately from the water; and behold, the heavens were opened, and he saw the Spirit of God descending as a dove *and* lighting on Him, [17]and behold, a voice out of the heavens said, 'This is My beloved Son, in whom I am well-pleased.'"

The Messiah will be a prophet like Moses.

Deuteronomy 18:15 "The Lord your God will raise up for you a prophet like me from among you, from your countrymen, you shall listen to him."

How was the prophecy fulfilled?

John 6:14 "Therefore when the people saw the sign which He had performed, they said, 'This is truly the Prophet who is to come into the world.'"

The Messiah will make the blind see, the deaf hear.

Isaiah 35:5 "Then the eyes of the blind will be opened And the ears of the deaf will be unstopped."

How was the prophecy fulfilled?

(Many scriptures show the fulfillment of this prophecy, but this is a particularly good one because it is an admission by his enemies.)

John 11:47 "Therefore the chief priests and the Pharisees convened a council, and were saying, 'What are we doing? For this man is performing many signs.'"

People will hate the Messiah without cause.

Psalm 69:4 "Those who hate me without a cause are more than the hairs of my head; Those who would destroy me are powerful, being wrongfully my enemies; What I did not steal, I then have to restore."

How was the prophecy fulfilled?

John 15:24-25 ²⁴"If I had not done among them the works which no one else did, they would not have sin; but now they have both seen and hated Me and My Father as well. ²⁵But *they have done this* to fulfill the word that is written in their Law, 'They hated Me without a cause.'"

The Messiah would be oppressed and afflicted, but would not open His mouth.

Isaiah 53:7 "He was oppressed and He was afflicted, Yet He did not open His mouth; Like a lamb that is led to slaughter, And like a sheep that is silent before its shearers, So He did not open His mouth."

How was the prophecy fulfilled?

Luke 23:8-11 ⁸"Now Herod was very glad when he saw Jesus; for he had wanted to see Him for a long time, because he had been hearing about Him and was hoping to see some sign performed by Him. ⁹And he questioned Him at some length; but He answered him nothing. ¹⁰And the chief priests and the scribes were standing there, accusing Him vehemently. ¹¹And Herod with his soldiers, after treating Him with contempt and mocking Him, dressed Him in a gorgeous robe and sent Him back to Pilate."

The Messiah will be plotted against by Jews and Gentiles together.

Psalm 2:1-2 [1]"Why are the nations in an uproar And the peoples devising a vain thing? [2]The kings of the earth take their stand and the rulers take counsel together against the Lord and against His Anointed,"

How was the prophecy fulfilled?

Acts 4:27-28 [27]"For truly in this city there were gathered together against Your holy servant Jesus, whom You anointed, both Herod and Pontius Pilate, along with the Gentiles and the peoples of Israel, [28]to do whatever Your hand and Your purpose predestined to occur."

The Messiah will be betrayed by a friend.

Psalm 41:9 "Even my close friend in whom I trusted, Who ate my bread, Has lifted up his heel against me."

How was the prophecy fulfilled?

Acts 1:16-17 [16]"Brethren, the Scripture had to be fulfilled, which the Holy Spirit foretold by the mouth of David concerning Judas, who became a guide to those who arrested Jesus. [17]For he was counted among us and received his share in this ministry."

The Messiah will be betrayed for 30 pieces of silver.

Zechariah 11:12 "I said to them, 'If it is good in your sight, give *me* my wages; but if not, never mind!' So they weighed out thirty *shekels* of silver as my wages."

How was the prophecy fulfilled?

Matthew 26:14-16   [14] Then one of the twelve, named Judas Iscariot, went to the chief priests [15]and said, "What are you willing to give me to betray Him to you?" And they weighed out thirty pieces of silver to him. [16]From then on he *began* looking for a good opportunity to betray Jesus.

The Messiah will have his price given for a potter's field.

Zechariah 11:13   "Then the Lord said to me, 'Throw it to the potter, *that* magnificent price at which I was valued by them.' So I took the thirty *shekels* of silver and threw them to the potter in the house of the Lord."

How was the prophecy fulfilled?

Matthew 27:6-7   [6]"The chief priests took the pieces of silver and said, 'It is not lawful to put them into the temple treasury, since it is the price of blood.' [7]And they conferred together and with the money bought the Potter's Field as a burial place for strangers."

The Messiah will be struck on the cheek.

Micah 5:1 "Now muster yourselves in troops, daughter of troops; They have laid siege against us; With a rod they will smite the judge of Israel on the cheek."

How was the prophecy fulfilled?

Matthew 27:30 "They spat on Him, and took the reed and *began* to beat Him on the head."

The Messiah's hands and feet will be pierced.

Psalm 22:16 "For dogs have surrounded me; A band of evildoers has encompassed me; They pierced my hands and my feet."

How was the prophecy fulfilled?

Luke 23:33 "When they came to the place called The Skull, there they crucified Him and the criminals, one on the right and the other on the left."

The Messiah will be beaten, mocked, and spat on.

Isaiah 50:6 "I gave My back to those who strike *Me*, And My cheeks to those who pluck out the beard; I did not cover My face from humiliation and spitting."

How was the prophecy fulfilled?

Matthew 27:30-31 [30]"They spat on Him, and took the reed and *began* to beat Him on the head. [31]After they had mocked Him, they took the *scarlet* robe off Him and put His *own* garments back on Him, and led Him away to crucify Him."

The Messiah will be given vinegar to quench His thirst.

Psalm 69:21 "They also gave me gall for my food And for my thirst they gave me vinegar to drink."

How was the prophecy fulfilled?

Matthew 27:34 "they gave Him wine to drink mixed with gall; and after tasting *it*, He was unwilling to drink."

When the Messiah dies, he will be buried with the rich.

Isaiah 53:9 "His grave was assigned with wicked men, Yet He was with a rich man in His death, Because He had done no violence, Nor was there any deceit in His mouth."

How was the prophecy fulfilled?

Matthew 27:57-60 [57]"When it was evening, there came a rich man from Arimathea, named Joseph, who himself had also become a disciple of Jesus. [58]This man went to Pilate and asked for the body of Jesus. Then Pilate ordered it to be given *to him*. [59]And Joseph took the body and wrapped it in a clean linen cloth, [60]and laid it in his own new tomb, which he had hewn out in the rock; and he rolled a large stone against the entrance of the tomb and went away."

We could look at many other prophecies. In total, Jesus fulfilled over 300 prophecies that appear in the Old Testament that were written hundreds of years before His birth. These 19 prophecies are mainly about the birth and death of Jesus. These were chosen because most of them involve the actions of others that would either be unaware of the prophecies; or the people would not have any interest in helping Jesus fulfill them; or they were prophecies fulfilled by situations that Jesus could not have manipulated in order to fulfill them.

The chances of a person fulfilling just these 19 prophecies we mention here out of the over 300 is astronomical. These prophecies are shared so that one may know Jesus is the Messiah.

> The chances of a person fulfilling just these 19 prophecies we mention here out of the over 300 is astronomical.

What Does Jesus Claim about Himself?

Chapter 7

We looked at what some outside of Christianity teach about Jesus. We looked at some of the Old Testament prophecies about Jesus. Now, let us look at what Jesus has to say about Himself. In his book, "Mere Christianity," C.S. Lewis writes,

> A man who was merely a man and said the sort of things Jesus said would not be a great moral teacher. He would either be a lunatic—on a level with the man who says he is a poached egg—or else he would be the Devil of Hell. You must make your choice. Either this man was, and is, the Son of God: or else a madman or something worse. You can shut Him up for a fool, you can spit at Him and kill Him as a demon; or you can fall at His feet and call Him Lord and God. But let us not come with any patronizing nonsense about His being a great human teacher. He has not left that open to us. He did not intend to.

"A man who was merely a man and said the sort of things Jesus said would not be a great moral teacher. He would either be a lunatic—on a level with the man who says he is a poached egg—or else he would be the Devil of Hell..."

Jesus claimed to live a sinless life.

John 8:28-29, 46-47 ²⁸"So Jesus said, 'When you lift up the Son of Man, then you will know that I am He, and I do nothing on My own initiative, but I speak these things as the Father taught Me. ²⁹And He who sent Me is with Me; He has not left Me alone, for I always do the things that are pleasing to Him.'"

⁴⁶"Which one of you convicts Me of sin? If I speak truth, why do you not believe Me? ⁴⁷He who is of God hears the words of God; for this reason you do not hear them, because you are not of God."

Jesus claimed to exist before Abraham.

John 8:56-58 ⁵⁶"Your father Abraham rejoiced to see My day, and he saw *it* and was glad." ⁵⁷So the Jews said to Him, "You are not yet fifty years old, and have You seen Abraham?" ⁵⁸Jesus said to them, "Truly, truly, I say to you, before Abraham was born, I am."

Jesus claimed to have shared the glory of God in Heaven before the world existed.

John 17:5 "Now, Father, glorify Me together with Yourself, with the glory which I had with You before the world was."

Jesus claimed to be able to forgive sins.

Luke 5:20-25 ²⁰Seeing their faith, He said, "Friend, your sins are forgiven you." ²¹The scribes and the Pharisees began to reason, saying, "Who is this *man* who speaks blasphemies? Who can forgive sins, but God alone?" ²²But Jesus, aware of their reasonings, answered and said to them, "Why are you reasoning in your hearts? ²³Which is easier, to say, 'Your sins have been forgiven you,' or to say, 'Get up and walk'? ²⁴But, so that you may know that the Son of Man has authority on earth to forgive sins,"—He said to the paralytic—"I say to you, get up, and pick up your stretcher and go home." ²⁵ Immediately he got up before them, and picked up what he had been lying on, and went home glorifying God.

Luke 7:48-49 ⁴⁸Then He said to her, "Your sins are forgiven." ⁴⁹And those who sat at the table with Him began to say to themselves, "Who is this who even forgives sins?"

Jesus claimed to be a heavenly king.

Luke 22:69 "But from now on the Son of Man will be seated at the right hand of the power of God."

John 18:36-37 ³⁶Jesus answered, "My kingdom is not of this world. If My kingdom were of this world, then My servants would be fighting so that I would not be handed over to the Jews; but as it is, My kingdom is not of this realm." ³⁷Therefore Pilate said to Him, "So You are a king?" Jesus answered, "You say *correctly* that I am a king. For this I have been born, and for this I have come into the world, to testify to the truth. Everyone who is of the truth hears My voice."

Jesus claimed to be able to give everlasting life.

John 6:40 – For this is the will of My Father, that everyone who beholds the Son and believes in Him will have eternal life, and I Myself will raise him up on the last day."

John 10:28-30 – and I give eternal life to them, and they will never perish; and no one will snatch them out of My hand. **29** My Father, who has given *them* to Me, is greater than all; and no one is able to snatch *them* out of the Father's hand. **30** I and the Father are one."

See also John 6:47 and John 11:25.

Jesus claimed that he would die and come back to life.

John 10:17-18 **17**"For this reason the Father loves Me, because I lay down My life so that I may take it again. **18**No one has taken it away from Me, but I lay it down on My own initiative. I have authority to lay it down, and I have authority to take it up again. This commandment I received from My Father."

Luke 18:32-33 **32**"For He will be handed over to the Gentiles, and will be mocked and mistreated and spit upon, **33**and after they have scourged Him, they will kill Him; and the third day He will rise again."

See also John 12:32-33 and John 16:16.

Jesus claimed that he would return to judge the world.

Matthew 24:29-30 **29**"But immediately after the tribulation of those days the sun will be darkened, and the moon will not give its light, and the stars will fall from the sky, and the powers of the heavens will be shaken. [30]And then the sign of the Son of Man will appear in the sky, and then all the tribes of the earth will mourn, and they will see the Son of Man coming on the clouds of the sky with power and great glory."

Matthew 25:31-32   [31]"But when the Son of Man comes in His glory, and all the angels with Him, then He will sit on His glorious throne. [32]All the nations will be gathered before Him; and He will separate them from one another, as the shepherd separates the sheep from the goats;"

Many people, including other world religions, teach Jesus was a good man, a teacher, and perhaps a prophet. However, when you realize that Jesus fulfilled over 300 prophecies written hundreds of years before His birth; and that He claimed to have an eternal existence, the power to forgive sins, to be one with God the Father, and the ability to grant others eternal life; then you should ask an important question. "Can this be just a good man, a teacher, or a prophet?"

Look at what Jesus says in John 5:39 about Himself. "You search the Scriptures because you think that in them you have eternal life; it is these that testify about Me;"

Jesus cannot be just a good man, a teacher, or a prophet. He must be the everlasting Son of God, the Lord of all creation, and the only Savior for mankind!

Jesus cannot be just a good man, a teacher, or a prophet. He must be the everlasting Son of God, the Lord of all creation, and the only Savior for mankind!

The Apostles

Chapter 8

What is the best proof that the claims Jesus made about Himself are the truth? To answer that, first read these scriptures.

Matthew 26:55-56 [55]"At that time Jesus said to the crowds, 'Have you come out with swords and clubs to arrest Me as *you would* against a robber? Every day I used to sit in the temple teaching and you did not seize Me. [56]But all this has taken place to fulfill the Scriptures of the prophets.' Then all the disciples left Him and fled."

John 18:16-17 [16]"but Peter was standing at the door outside. So the other disciple, who was known to the high priest, went out and spoke to the doorkeeper, and brought Peter in. [17]Then the slave-girl who kept the door said to Peter, 'You are not also *one* of this man's disciples, are you?' He said, 'I am not.'"

John 20:19 "So when it was evening on that day, the first *day* of the week, and when the doors were shut where the disciples were, for fear of the Jews, Jesus came and stood in their midst and said to them, 'Peace *be* with you.'"

Why did I show you these scriptures? So that you may see that the apostles were a bunch of spineless wimps, cowards, and depressed. Then, what happened? These whimpering men, bound the Roman soldiers, rolled the three-ton boulder away from Jesus' grave, and stole the body? Well, only a fool would believe that. These men were despondent and broken.

The best proof of the authenticity of Jesus' claims is that He resurrected from the dead. The best evidence of His resurrection is the changed lives of the apostles.

How did the apostles change, you ask? The changes were miraculous indeed.

The apostles began praising God in the temple.

Luke 24:52-53   52"And they, after worshiping Him, returned to Jerusalem with great joy, 53and were continually in the temple praising God."

The apostles began proclaiming Christ, despite persecution.

Acts 5:27-29   27"When they had brought them, they stood them before the Council. The high priest questioned them, saying, 'We gave you strict orders not to continue teaching in this name, and yet, you have filled Jerusalem with your teaching and intend to bring this man's blood upon us.' 29But Peter and the apostles answered, 'We must obey God rather than men.'"

1 Corinthians 4:9-13   9"For, I think, God has exhibited us apostles last of all, as men condemned to death; because we have become a spectacle to the world, both to angels and to men. 10We are fools for Christ's sake, but you are prudent in Christ; we are weak, but you are strong; you are distinguished, but we are without honor. 11To this present hour we are both hungry and thirsty, and are poorly clothed, and are roughly treated, and are homeless; 12and we toil, working with our own hands; when we

are reviled, we bless; when we are persecuted, we endure; [13]when we are slandered, we try to conciliate; we have become as the scum of the world, the dregs of all things, *even* until now."

The once spineless Apostles were willing to die a martyr's death.

Acts 12:1-2 [1]"Now about that time Herod the king laid hands on some who belonged to the church in order to mistreat them. [2]And he had James the brother of John put to death with a sword."

What about the other apostles? How did they die? Most died a martyr's death. However, after failing to kill John by plunging him into boiling oil, he was banished to the island of Patmos, where he died of old age.

Question: Who dies for what they know to be a lie?

Answer: NO ONE!

A Personal Relationship

Chapter 9

You might be thinking, "I know there is a God, but how can I develop that relationship to God you mentioned earlier?" On our own, this would be impossible. The bad news is we are all separated from God because of our sin. We are not children of God, just because we have been born. But we can be adopted into His family if we choose.

First, we must understand that according to the Bible, we are all sinners. Romans 3:23 tells us that all have sinned and fall short of the glory of God. If you tell one lie, you fall short of God's requirement of perfection.

We must also realize that the penalty of sin is death, but that God has provided a plan of redemption for us. In Romans 6:23 we read God's warning that the wages of sin is death, but that the free gift of God is eternal life through His son Christ Jesus.

God's standard of perfection is what He requires in order to enter heaven. John tells us in Revelation 21:27 that nothing unclean, and no one who practices abomination and lying, shall ever come into it, but only those whose names are written in the Lamb's book of life.

> We must also realize that the penalty of sin is death, but that God has provided a plan of redemption for us.

Have you ever told a lie? Then, according to God Word, you are not worthy of being called a child of God or of entering heaven. However, don't despair! I have good news!

2 Corinthians 5:21 "He made Him who knew no sin *to be* sin on our behalf, so that we might become the righteousness of God in Him."

We see in this verse that Jesus offers us *His* righteousness. And Ephesians 2:8-9 reiterates to us that it is a gift, not something we can earn or buy. [8]"For by grace you have been saved through faith; and that not of yourselves, *it is* the gift of God; [9] not as a result of works, so that no one may boast."

> 2 Corinthians 5:21 "He made Him who knew no sin to be sin on our behalf, so that we might become the righteousness of God in Him."

You see we simply need to repent (understand the direction we were heading without God and change our minds about our sin) and trust in the Lord Jesus Christ as our savior for salvation. It is something God wants for all of us. 2 Peter 3:9 "The Lord is not slow about His promise, as some count slowness, but is patient toward you, not wishing for any to perish but for all to come to repentance." It is a gift, and all we need to do is accept it. These next verses tell us how.

Romans 10:9-10   ⁹"that if you confess with your mouth Jesus *as* Lord, and believe in your heart that God raised Him from the dead, you will be saved; ¹⁰for with the heart a person believes, resulting in righteousness, and with the mouth he confesses, resulting in salvation."

We can be sure of our eternal salvation. God, our loving Abba Father promises that no one can ever take this away from us; therefore, we are assured we cannot lose it.

John 10:28-29   ²⁸"and I give eternal life to them, and they will never perish; and no one will snatch them out of My hand. ²⁹My Father, who has given *them* to Me, is greater than all; and no one is able to snatch *them* out of the Father's hand."

The most quoted verse in the Bible is John 3:16. "For God so loved the world, that He gave His only begotten Son, that whoever believes in Him shall not perish, but have eternal life."

Does that verse say, "whosoever believeth and behaves," or "whosoever believeth and does good works," or "whosoever believeth and goes to confession"? No, and a few chapters later, when people are asking Jesus about salvation, he again makes it quite clear in John 6:28-29.

²⁸"Therefore they said to Him, 'What shall we do, so that we may work the works of God?' ²⁹Jesus answered and said to them, 'This is the work of God, that you believe in Him whom He has sent.'"

They asked Jesus about "works," but Jesus responded using the singular word "work." This is because there is nothing more to do.

Salvation is completely by grace alone, through Christ alone, for the glory of God alone. The moment you think there are things you must do to be saved or stay saved; you are removing the glory from God.

To drive this point home, I will illustrate using an object we are all familiar with, a chair. We sit on them every day without a second thought. We never cautiously examine them before we sit down; we sit without thinking about it.

So, let me ask you a question, at what point are you fully trusting in the chair to hold you up? If I squat down and very carefully place one half of one side of my derrière on the corner of the chair, am I demonstrating trust in the chair to hold me up? What if I keep some of my weight on my left leg, and while leaning on my left leg, I carefully slide over to place a little more weight on the chair? Am I then trusting in the chair *alone* to support me? What if I slide over even more so that my whole backside and thighs are over the chair, but I am leaning forward with my hands on my knees and keeping some weight over my feet? Am I trusting *fully* in the chair to hold me? What if I now stand on the chair with both feet? Have I put full confidence in the chair to support me? Yes, unquestionably, if I am standing on the chair, I have completely trusted in the chair to hold me.

Let's look again at Ephesians 2:8-9, "For by grace [undeserved favor] you have been saved [delivered from sin's penalty] through faith, and that not of yourselves; it is the gift of God, not as a result of works, so that no one may boast."

The word faith means "trust."

For what must you trust Christ? You must depend on Him alone to forgive you and to give you eternal life. Just as you trust a chair to hold you through no effort of your own, so you must trust Jesus Christ to get you to heaven through no effort of your own. Salvation is not gained through good works, nor by faith in Christ

> For what must you trust Christ? You must depend on Him alone to forgive you and to give you eternal life.

plus good works. Salvation is placing your full trust in Christ alone to save you.

Now let's take a closer look at John 10:28-29.

[28]"and I give eternal life to them, and they will never perish; and no one will snatch them out of My hand. [29]My Father, who has given *them* to Me, is greater than all; and no one is able to snatch *them* out of the Father's hand."

"And I give . . ." Have you ever given something to someone? Did you expect something in return? What is the gift here? The gift is eternal salvation. When does Jesus give the gift? Is it when they perish? Is it when they sin again? No. it is immediately given to those who turn to Jesus Christ.

Whose hand are we in when we trust in Christ? We are in God the Father's hands. Who can remove us from those hands? The Almighty, all-powerful God of the universe declares that no one can take us out of His hands. When we put our trust in Christ, we *have; not will have; not have if* enough people pray us out of purgatory, eternal life, and our salvation is secure.

When we trust Christ, many things take place. Here are some of them:

1. We are forgiven of all sin.

Colossians 2:13 "When you were dead in your transgressions and the uncircumcision of your flesh, He made you alive together with Him, having forgiven us all our transgressions,"

How many transgressions? All. What about the transgressions you commit after trusting in Christ? All means all.

2. We receive eternal life.

John 3:36 "He who believes in the Son has eternal life; but he who does not obey the Son will not see life, but the wrath of God abides on him."

1 John 5:11, 13 [11]"And the testimony is this, that God has given us eternal life, and this life is in His Son. [13]These things I have written to you who believe in the name of the Son of God, so that you may know that you have eternal life.

When do we receive the gift of eternal life? When we trust Christ or when we die? We have eternal life the moment we trust in Christ, and nothing can take it away.

3. We have freedom from condemnation.

John 5:24 "Truly, truly, I say to you, he who hears My word, and believes Him who sent Me, has eternal life, and does not come into judgment, but has passed out of death into life."

Romans 8:1 "Therefore there is now no condemnation for those who are in Christ Jesus."

When we trust in Christ, we are fully pardoned. We cannot be held guilty for our sins.

4. We are justified; meaning, we are declared righteous by God.

Romans 5:1 "Therefore, having been justified by faith, we have peace with God through our Lord Jesus Christ,"

We have justification and peace with God. How many of us would love to have instant peace with some family members here on Earth? When we trust in Christ, we instantly have peace with God. AMEN!

5. We receive the Holy Spirit.

1 Corinthians 12:13 "For by one Spirit we were all baptized into one body, whether Jews or Greeks, whether slaves or free, and we were all made to drink of one Spirit."

Ephesians 1:12-13   [12]"to the end that we who were the first to hope in Christ would be to the praise of His glory. [13]In Him, you also, after listening to the message of truth, the gospel of your salvation — having also believed, you were sealed in Him with the Holy Spirit of promise,"

We become indwelt with and sealed by the Holy Spirit. And here are two more things we become.

6. We become a new creature in Christ Jesus.

2 Corinthians 5:17 "Therefore if anyone is in Christ, *he is* a new creature; the old things passed away; behold, new things have come."

We are a new creature that has a new conscience, and our lives are no longer just worldly. We have a new spiritual nature. Our old sin nature which God placed on Christ at the cross has been crucified. God buried our sin with Jesus, and just as the Father raised Jesus, so are we raised to "walk in newness of life." Yes, we still have a fleshly nature, and must choose daily which nature to follow—the old or the new. That is why as long as we live in our imperfect mortal bodies, we will sin again. The difference is we also have a new spiritual nature that pricks our conscience when we sin and helps us to live for God.

7. We become a child of God.

John 1:12 "But as many as received Him, to them He gave the right to become children of God, *even* to those who believe in His name,"

Romans 8:14-16 [14]"For all who are being led by the Spirit of God, these are sons of God. [15]For you have not received a spirit of slavery leading to fear again, but you have received a spirit of adoption as sons by which we cry out, "Abba! Father!" [16]The Spirit Himself testifies with our spirit that we are children of God,"

Once we trust in Christ, we are a child of God and can find our security in Him.

Let's look at Galatians 3:1-3 to give us one final illustration of grace and to make this abundantly clear.

Galatians 3:1-3 [1]"You foolish Galatians, who has bewitched you, before whose eyes Jesus Christ was publicly portrayed *as* crucified? [2]This is the only thing I want to find out from you: did you receive the Spirit by the works of the Law, or by hearing with faith? [3]Are you so foolish? Having begun by the Spirit, are you now being perfected by the flesh?

Why are these Galatians being chastised? Because these Christians were living a legalistic life, thinking they must do certain things to remain a Christian. But they were creating a religion of works. As we have already studied, once we are in Christ's hands, once the Spirit seals us, our sin-debt is paid in full. There is nothing more to do.

Now God does give us instruction on how to live, yes, but we follow His instruction out of love and thankfulness for Him. He gave us a standard to live by, and we should hold to that standard out of love and respect for Him because He has saved us from our sin, but not in order to keep our salvation.

Jesus will never leave us or forsake us. He will never hate us or show us a lack of love. He will correct us and guide us because He loves us.

> ...once we are in Christ's hands, once the Spirit seals us, our sin-debt is paid in full. There is nothing more to do.

God has corrected my path and guided me in various ways over the years. One such time he corrected my path was when I was a freshman in college. I had just completed my first semester and decided college was not yet for me. I wanted to join the Air Force. So, I went and talked to an Air Force recruiter. I took the ASVAB test and did very well. The recruiter told me I could have just about any Air Force job I wanted.

Two weeks before I was supposed to go and sign my life away, the recruiter called me.

"Mr. Wells, I am sorry to inform you that you do not qualify to join the Air Force."

"I don't understand, sir. You said I would be eligible for just about any position in the Air Force I wanted."

"That was before going over your medical records which indicate that you have a heart condition, Mr. Wells."

"Heart condition? I have no idea what you're talking about. I have never even had my heart examined, sir."

"Well then, Mr. Wells, you will need to go and get a heart test done. If everything checks out, we will still take you."

So, my dad took me to the university hospital, and they ran tests on my heart, and I got to see my heart pumping on a television screen. It was impressive to see this. Well, I passed all the tests, but it began to bother me that I even needed to take them. I wondered what was on my medical records and why?

About this time, God began to show me that everything I did was because I thought it was a good idea. I was not allowing God to be part of my decision-making process. Who knows me completely? Who knows me better than I know myself? I knew that God did. I had great parents and a relationship with my heavenly Father, yet I was acting alone.

For the first time, I started to pray about this. Then, it was as if God was audibly speaking to me. I felt a calming, quiet peace that the reason the recruiter saw what he saw on my records was that God wanted me to go in a different direction. I called the recruiter and informed him I was not going to pursue a career in the Air Force any longer.

> Then, it was as if God was audibly speaking to me. I felt a calming, quiet peace that the reason the recruiter saw what he saw on my records was that God wanted me to go in a different direction.

Instead, that summer through my involvement with InterVarsity Christian Fellowship, I went on an evangelism project with 30 other college students to Aspen, Colorado. InterVarsity students went there from all over the western United States. We were in Aspen to minister to the international music students that stay in Aspen every summer for international music festivals.

To cut the story short, one of the InterVarsity students that came with a group from Texas became my wife, Maria. You see, had I gone to the Air Force, I would not have met Maria, and I would not have my four beautiful kids.

Let me share one more personal story of how my heavenly Father gave me clear guidance in making a significant decision that would impact me and my family's lives.

In the year 2007, my wife and I and our children were living in the southern tip of Texas, the Rio Grande Valley, just east of McAllen, Texas. That is the area where my wife grew up. We attended a weekend marriage conference at our church that was taught by Dr. Stan Ponz, then Senior Pastor at International Church of Oahu.

During that weekend, Pastor Stan mentioned he was looking for five leaders willing to move to Hawaii. His statement tickled my ear a little, but not much else. The conference ended, Pastor Stan went back to Hawaii, and life continued as before. However, I kept in contact with him, and eventually, I started asking him questions about what he meant that he was looking for Christian leaders to move to Hawaii. I began to wonder if perhaps God would like for us to move there, if maybe just maybe that was part of my calling. I had conversations with my wife and kids about the idea. Now, let me tell you, they were not exactly excited about the idea of moving so far away.

My oldest daughter was in an excellent school, and she was immensely serious about her academics. I mean, she was a straight-A student. So, I began talking to her about the prospect of moving, and I mentioned to her that I am sure Hawaii has some good schools. Then, she said something that became like the fleece was to Gideon.

I am referring to Gideon's request to God found in Judges 6:36-40. God had asked Gideon to fight the Midianites. Gideon asks God for a sign to confirm God's will to him. He asks God to make his fleece garment on the ground wet, but to keep the ground dry. Then, he reversed that and asked God to make the ground wet and to keep the fleece dry. Well, my daughter's response became my test, my fleece.

When I told her that I was sure Hawaii must have some excellent schools, she told me, "Yes, but not an IB school." Now, that might not sound like much to you, but let me explain. When she said IB, she meant, a school that offered an International Baccalaureate program. The IB Foundation sets high international academic standards, and students that graduate having met those standards receive an IB diploma. Such a diploma looks impressive to college administrators.

She already attended a charter school that met this standard, and she wanted to continue to attend a school that offered the IB curriculum; and thus, give her an opportunity to achieve the coveted IB diploma. In reality, my daughter was not very fond of the idea of moving and was sure Hawaii would not have an IB school.

I decided to research the IB web site's list of schools. I discovered that at that time, Hawaii had two IB schools. Both schools were on

Oahu — one private and one public. I knew we could not afford private school, so I sought more information on the public school, James Campbell.

At that time, I knew nothing about Hawaii. I did not even know how many islands there were. About all I knew was it was somewhere in the Pacific. I did not even know on which island Pastor Stan lived. This prompted a phone call to him.

"Pastor Stan, can you tell me anything about James Campbell High School? Is it on the same island you live on?"

"Oh, yes, Scott, it is here on Oahu. It is a good school. It is in Ewa Beach on the west side of the island, which would be a great area to have a ministry."

I was so excited I could hardly contain myself. I could now see the hand of God directing our family toward Hawaii. It was 2008, and Maria and I decided we should check out Hawaii and see if we could live there. We took two weeks to visit Hawaii that summer. While on Oahu, we fell in love with the people and the culture and saw God's hand leading us to Hawaii.

I started applying for jobs, but nothing came through while we were visiting Hawaii. We went back home and using online job sites I continued to look for work on Oahu. There were several jobs I was very well qualified to do as a Systems Administrator, and I applied for all of them. However, in spite of being well qualified for all of these positions, I was not hired by any of the companies. The typical reason I was given was because I was not there, and they wanted to hire someone that already lived in Hawaii.

I did not understand. I talked to God. "God, it seems like you want us to move to Hawaii, but how can we move if I don't even have a job?"

I had been reading from the book of Joshua chapter 3. It seemed God was teaching me from the example in Scripture and speaking to my heart.

"Do you see the step of faith the Israelites took by stepping out into the flooding Jordan River in obedience to my command? They trusted Me, and I stopped the water for My people to safely cross. Scott, that is what I need you to do. You need to take a step of faith."

I knew the story of Joshua leading the Israelites across the Jordan River as recorded in Joshua 3 in the Old Testament. I knew that indeed God did protect and provide for Joshua and the Israelites as they trusted God. The question was, "Was I willing to take a step of faith like that to lead my family?"

I told Maria, my wife, about my prayer, devotions, and thoughts from the Lord. We discussed me going to Hawaii by myself, getting a job, and finding a place to live. Then she and the kids could move to join me once school was out for the summer. It was early 2009, and I started looking for plane tickets and planning my trip. I decided that the best thing for me to do was to pack my van, drive to my mom's house in Arizona, have my van shipped from there, and fly out from Arizona. It was a little cheaper to ship from Arizona, and I would see my family before moving to Hawaii.

Doubts started coming back into my mind. Could I really afford the move? I prayed and asked God to provide the way. Out of nowhere, I received a check in the mail. This check was to the dollar the price of the plane tickets I had seen online! There was just an 11 cents difference, and I told God I could cover the 11 cents. To this day, I cannot fully explain that check.

I purchased the ticket, packed my things in the van, and got on my way. At that point, I had committed to God's leading and had taken the first steps of moving to Hawaii. I was halfway to Tucson, in the middle of the New Mexico desert, when my cell phone rang. It was the IT manager at Easterseals Hawaii to whom I had previously spoken. He had interviewed me over the phone, but after weeks passed, I had never given it a second thought.

The manager told me that he was interested in me being their Systems Administrator and asked if I could be there by April 6th. I told him yes that I was flying in on the 5th. He said, "Good because I want you here for a final interview." That person became my boss. You see, it was just like the Jews taking a step of faith and walking into the Jordan River before God stopped the water. God wanted me to act, to trust Him. He wanted me to get on my way, and then He blessed me with the job I was searching for.

Your Relationship with God

Where are you in your spiritual walk? Maybe you trusted Christ years ago, but you have not really developed a close walk with God. Maybe you still feel some distance between you and the God of the universe who is also your Abba Father. Let me say that it is not God who is keeping His distance. If you trusted in Jesus, then you are still in His hand. He is the one knocking on the door to your life and saying, "Let Me be part of every aspect of your life. Allow Me to guide every decision you make. Let Me hold you when the going gets tough. Trust Me not just for salvation, but to help you in every area of your life."

Now maybe you are asking the questions, "How do I do that? How can I draw closer to God as my Abba Father, literally our Heavenly Daddy?"

Step 1: Develop a Healthy Devotional Life

- Set a regular time to read and meditate on Scripture.

- Include time for worshiping God and giving Him thanks for His many blessings.

- Spend time in prayer and intercession not only for yourself and your family but also for friends, the church, the cause of Christ in world missions, the lost, the government.

- Set a time daily, a "date" with God, for reflection, for confessing sin, and communing with God.

Step 2: Develop a Healthy Church Life

- Realize that developing as a Christian is not a solo performance.

- Know the Holy Spirit desires you to partner with other Christians in an organized body of believers, to help us in our spiritual walk.

- Be reminded that a significant purpose of the church is the "building up" of believers and spiritual growth, just as Paul often wrote to churches in the New Testament.

Step 3: Develop a Healthy Small Group Life

- Unique benefits come to God's people meeting in smaller groups, benefits not available within a large group. If a Sunday school class or a Bible study group is small enough and interactive, it can provide mutual support and accountability.

- People grow through relating in small groups as evidenced by their comments.

  - "They know me personally."

  - "They know where I'm coming from."

  - "I've gotten personal encouragement from these close Christian friends."

  - "The instruction fit my circumstances."

  - "It's comforting to see that others wrestle with the same problems I do."

Step 4: Develop a Healthy One-to-One Relationship with Another Christian

- One-to-one relationships are even more personalized than the small group.

- A regular "prayer buddy" or partner with whom you can share freely can help your spiritual walk.

- Be open with this person and share your spiritual struggles.

- This person should be of the same gender.

Step 5: Develop a Habit of Sharing Christ with Others

Sharing Christ is simple. Just keep in mind everyone needs to know two things, they are sinners who need saving, and God provided that Savior. Here are some basic points to keep in mind when sharing God's love to a person that does not know Him.

- People, in general, do not understand God's standards. They consider themselves to be good.

- A typical response to the question, "Do you know that you will go to heaven when you die?" is, "I think I am a pretty good person, and I will get there because I am not a bad person."

- Many individuals have no idea they are drowning in sin and need salvation. So, once you turn the conversation toward spiritual matters, the first step in sharing the gospel is revealing to them their sinful condition.

- Help them understand that because God is Holy, God's standard is perfection, and all of us fall short of that mark with verses like Romans 3:23 which illustrate that we are all sinners.

- Show them Romans 6:23 which tells us that the wages of sin is death.

- Explain that because of our sin, we have earned death, eternal separation from God, and there is nothing we can do to overcome our sin and pay our sin debt.

- Then show them how much God loves them and wants to show them grace and mercy with verses like Romans 5:8, 2 Corinthians 5:21, Ephesians 2:8-9, and John 3:16.

- Once you have shown them these two things — helping them see they are sinners who need saving, and that there is a loving Savior who can rescue them — then ask them this question. "Would you like to trust Christ right now to be your savior?"

- If they are not sure or say no, then give them a piece of paper and ask them to write down five things that are keeping them from putting their trust in Christ. Writing things down will help them think things through.

Once you trust Christ, develop your relationship by following five steps:
1: Develop a Healthy Devotional Life
2: Develop a Healthy Church Life
3: Develop a Healthy Small Group Life
4: Develop a Healthy One-to-One Relationship with Another Christian
5: Develop a Habit of Sharing Christ with Others

You may be thinking, "Yeah, but what if I don't know how to address the things they wrote down?" Well, fantastic, that gives you another reason to meet with them again. Let them know you will find out these answers and get back to them. Do not be afraid of questions. Questions are simply opportunities for you to either answer on the spot or to arrange another meeting while you find answers.

Sharing the good news of the gospel is simple. We need to do it and let God take care of their response.

An Encouraging Closing

Once you trust Christ, your salvation is secure. But that is just the beginning of your understanding and your relationship to God. Remember, to grow as God's child, take these five steps developing: a healthy devotional life, a healthy church life, a healthy small group life, a healthy one-to-one relationship with another Christian, and a habit of sharing Christ with others. You absolutely will blossom as a Christian. You will grow closer to God than you ever thought possible. You will see God, the King of Kings and Lord of Lords, as your Heavenly Daddy, perhaps as the daddy you never had, and you will enjoy an incredibly special and everlasting relationship with God! AMEN!

References

1. Star Formation. (n.d.). Retrieved June 1, 2018, from
    http://abyss.uoregon.edu/~js/ast122/lectures/lec13.html

2. Howell, E. (2017, May 18). How Many Stars Are In The Universe?
    Retrieved June 3, 2018, from https://www.space.com/26078-
    how-many-stars-are-there.html

3. Choi, C. Q. (2016, March 24). 7 Theories on the Origin of Life.
    Retrieved June 1, 2018, from http://www.livescience.com/13363-
    7-theories-origin-life.html

4. Paul Davies, Australian Centre for Astrobiology, Macquarie
    University, Sydney. New Scientist 179(2403);32 12 July, 2003

5. (2004, November). Discover, 64.

6. Is the Moon Really Old? (1992, September 1). Retrieved June 9,
    2018, from https://answersingenesis.org/astronomy/moon/is-
    the-moon-really-old/

7. Powell, D. (2007, January 22). Earth's Moon Destined to
    Disintegrate. Retrieved June 8, 2018, from
    https://www.space.com/3373-earth-moon-destined-
    disintegrate.html

8. Is the Moon Really Old? (1992, September 1). Retrieved June 9,
    2018, from https://answersingenesis.org/astronomy/moon/is-
    the-moon-really-old/

9. Cook, M. A. (1966). Prehistory and earth models. London:
    Parrish. pp. 253-262.

10. US Department of Commerce, & National Oceanic and
    Atmospheric Administration. (2008, November 14). Why
    is the ocean salty? Retrieved July 5, 2018, from
    https://oceanservice.noaa.gov/facts/whysalty.html

11. US Department of Commerce, & National Oceanic and Atmospheric Administration. (2013, June 1). Why do we have oceans? Retrieved July 5, 2018, from https://oceanservice.noaa.gov/facts/why_oceans.html

12. S.A. Austin and D.R. Humphreys, "The sea's missing salt: a dilemma for evolutionists," Proceedings of the Second International Conference on Creationism, Vol. II, pp. 17-33, 1990

13. Florida Retina Institute. (n.d.). For Patients. Retrieved February 3, 2017, from https://www.floridaretinainstitute.com/fun-eye-facts.html

14. Sherwin, F. (n.d.). Cells: Sophisticated and God-Designed. Retrieved August 1, 2018, from https://www.icr.org/article/cells-sophisticated-god-designed

15. Gracepoint Forum. (n.d.). Retrieved June 20, 2018, from http://www.gracepointforum.org/2009/07/

16. Miller, H. S. (1960). General biblical introduction. Word-Bearen Press. p.6

17. Thiessen, H. C. (1977). Introductory lectures in systematic theology. Grand Rapids, MI: Eerdmans. p.79

18. Chafer, L. S., Walvoord, J. F., Campbell, D. K., & Zuck, R. B. (1988). Systematic theology (Vol. I). Dallas, TX.: Dallas Seminary Press.

19. GUTHRIE, J. L. (n.d.). Welcome to DiscoverTheWordWithDrJim.com. Retrieved September 7, 2018, from http://discoverthewordwithdrjim.com/guthrie/creation/CHAPTER_IV.html

20. McDowell, J. (2018, October 2). Is the Bible Reliable. Retrieved November 30, 2018, from https://www.josh.org/resurrection/is-the-bible-reliable/

21. F.F. Bruce - Frederick Fyvie Bruce. (n.d.). Retrieved from https://www.ffbruce.com/his-fundamentals/

22. Richison, G. (n.d.). Daniel 11:2-4. Retrieved September 14, 2018, from https://versebyversecommentary.com/daniel/daniel-112-4/

23. Mark 15:25 (cf. John 19:14)-Was Jesus crucified in the third hour or the sixth hour? (2015, January 1). Retrieved August 12, 2018, from https://defendinginerrancy.com/bible-solutions/Mark_15.25_(cf._John_19.14).php

24. GotQuestions.org. (2008, May 4). Home. Retrieved October 21, 2018, from https://www.gotquestions.org/blood-water-Jesus.html

All quotes from the Bible are from the New American Standard unless otherwise noted.

About the author:

Scott Wells is an International speaker and teacher. From his youth, he has had a passion for Christian apologetics. He has studied much on creation science, evolutionary science, bibliology, and how we can know the Truth. He has studied and taught courses from fantastic organizations such as Answers in Genesis, Living Waters and Creation Today. Also, the man whose work is most responsible for him going down this road is the founder of the Institute for Creation Research, Dr. Henry Morris, Ph.D. Many consider Dr. Morris to be "the father of modern creation science." If this is a subject that interests you, Scott would recommend any of his books. It is Scott's deepest desire to share the knowledge that he has gained with the world. We hope this book blesses you.

www.ingramcontent.com/pod-product-compliance
Lightning Source LLC
Chambersburg PA
CBHW060114050426
42448CB00010B/1864